PENGUIN PASSNOTES
KES

Susan Quilliam was born in Liverpool and read
Psychology and English at Liverpool University. After a
period of teaching she moved to London where she now
works as a freelance writer, as well as a counsellor. She
has written a number of study guides in the Penguin
Passnotes series, including *Pride and Prejudice*, *Silas
Marner* and *A Taste of Honey*, and is the author of
Positive Smear (Penguin 1989).

PENGUIN PASSNOTES

KES

Originally published as
A Kestrel for a Knave

SUSAN QUILLIAM
ADVISORY EDITOR: S. H. COOTE, M.A., PH.D.

PENGUIN BOOKS

PENGUIN BOOKS

Published by the Penguin Group
27 Wrights Lane, London W8 5TZ, England
Viking Penguin Inc., 40 West 23rd Street, New York, New York 10010, USA
Penguin Books Australia Ltd, Ringwood, Victoria, Australia
Penguin Books Canada Ltd, 2801 John Street, Markham, Ontario, Canada L3R 1B4
Penguin Books (NZ) Ltd, 182–190 Wairau Road, Auckland 10, New Zealand

Penguin Books Ltd, Registered Offices: Harmondsworth, Middlesex, England

First published 1986
10 9 8 7 6 5 4 3

Interactive approach developed by Susan Quilliam

Made and printed in Great Britain by
Richard Clay Ltd, Bungay, Suffolk
Filmset in Monophoto Ehrhardt

Contents

Acknowledgements

For permission to reproduce copyright material grateful acknowledgement is made to the following: B. T. Batsford Ltd for an extract from *Falconry in Mews and Field* by Emma Ford; Faber and Faber Ltd for 'The Hawk in the Rain' by Ted Hughes from *The Hawk in the Rain* and for 'The Bird' by Edwin Muir from *The Collected Poems of Edwin Muir*; David Higham Associates Ltd for an extract from *The Goshawk* by T. H. White, published by Jonathan Cape Ltd; Northern House Ltd for 'Buzzard Soaring' by Roger Garfitt from *The Broken Road*.

To the Student

The purpose of this book is to help you appreciate Barry Hines's novel *Kes*. It will help you to understand details of the plot. It will also help you to think about the characters, about what the writer is trying to say and how he says it. These things are most important. After all, understanding and responding to plots, characters and ideas are what make books come alive for us.

You will find this Passnote most useful after you have read *Kes* through at least once. A first reading will reveal the plot and make you think about the lives of the people it describes and your feelings for them. Now your job will be to make those first impressions clear. You will need to read the book again and ask yourself some questions. What does the writer really mean? What do I think about this incident or that one? How does the writer make such and such a character come alive?

This Passnote has been designed to help you do this. It offers you background information. It also asks many questions. You may like to write answers to some of these. Others you can answer in your head. The questions are meant to make you think, feel and respond. As you answer them, you will gain a clearer knowledge of the book and of your own ideas about it. When your thoughts are indeed clear, then you will be able to write confidently because you have made yourself an alert and responsive reader.

An Interview with Barry Hines

Barry Hines is to be found tucked away in a modern office on the campus of Sheffield Polytechnic. He doesn't work there officially now but, 'They like having writers around . . .' He seems in his mid-forties, is slim, wears glasses and talks with a Yorkshire accent. He's very easy to talk to, open and enthusiastic about everything I want to know.

Why did he write *Kes* in the first place? A sigh tells me that he has been asked this many times. 'There's no simple answer . . . I write about issues.' The issue that *Kes* deals with, it seems, is the education system. An emphatic nod, and a clenched fist drums on the table top. 'I don't like what it does to kids like Billy.'

The emotion there makes me ask if Billy Casper is really Barry Hines in disguise. Are we reading about his own childhood, his own experience? The answer is a mixture of yes and no. 'Billy isn't me. I wasn't too academic, but I did go to grammar school; I wasn't raised in a broken home, but in a loving, working-class family.'

Even so, there is a great deal of Barry Hines's own experience in the book. The small village where he was brought up, Hoyland Common, is set in Yorkshire countryside. Barry, like Billy, knew both the life of a mining community and the life of the wild.

The school in *Kes* is also taken directly from personal experience, from stories Barry heard each day from friends and family about a nearby secondary modern school: 'A circus – an absolute circus.' Everything he describes in *Kes* happened, says Barry, and the tales he didn't include in the book are the ones no one would believe. 'The headmaster once caned an electrician by mistake . . .'

What about his own experience in teaching? After six months down the pits and an attempt to become a professional footballer – he still fanatically supports West Ham United – he trained as a P.E. teacher at Loughborough Training College ('There's a lot of Farthing in me') and he taught English occasionally ('But a lot of Sugden too'). He laughs ruefully. 'The bits about Sugden are my apology to the kids I made stand in goal every lesson.' I get the impression he's being a bit hard on himself.

What about Kes? Surely Barry Hines himself didn't train a kestrel? Again the nod. 'My brother did – and I helped him.' As teenagers both Barry and his brother Richard kept and trained animals ('magpies, jackdaws'), just as Barry describes in the book. But Barry fought shy of hawks, feeling they were too difficult to handle, even though he knew that nearby, in a ruined hall, the original of Monastery Farm, there was a kestrel's nest.

At eighteen, though, with the help of a builder's ladder – the climb as described in the book never happened, for the wall was dangerously decayed – Richard Hines took a kestrel and trained it up. 'They've made it illegal now, and quite right too.' Barry, now living in his own house nearby, helped, keeping the hawk in the shed at the bottom of his garden, feeding it, flying it when his brother couldn't. They were inspired and helped by the *The Goshawk* by T. H. White, bought on the cheap when a private library sold off its books. Was training the hawk difficult? Yes, but not impossible, and very rewarding. Barry Hines's eyes light up as he remembers flying the bird.

So is that why he had Billy train a kestrel? 'Well – it's a subject I know about, so it was natural for me to choose it.' But, it seems, it could have been a motorbike that Billy was interested in and good at riding. The point is that, once motivated, Billy changes.

Is Billy a real person? No, though certainly a realistic one who snivels, tells lies, is in trouble with the police: not a hero. Barry Hines laughs at that. He says he's taught plenty of lads like Billy who have talent and strength but of the sort that isn't recognized at school or at home. 'People think you're not worth anything unless you've got qualifications.' The fist descends on the table top again to emphasize the injustice of it all. Barry Hines has also taught boys from broken homes – 'I made Billy's home like that because it gives him no let-up from what he's going through.'

And the other characters? He's known them all – or, rather, bits and pieces of them. Only Gryce is a real person, a headmaster Barry once knew. The others – Jud, Mrs Casper, the teachers and shopkeepers – are taken from here and there, characters built up to show the good and the bad. Barry Hines feels that these characters are simplified; Billy is the important one. That's the way he always writes. 'I concentrate on one main character – everything else goes into black and white.'

What about the language of the book? Barry Hines talks of the importance of real-life language. 'Don't call horses "steeds" just because you're writing a book.' He certainly follows this through, speaking strongly and clearly about what he's done, seen, heard, particularly about what he believes, in just the same way as he writes.

The conversation begins to turn from the past to the present. I'm interested to know if, given the chance to write *Kes* again now, Barry Hines would change anything. A pause for thought, then, 'It'd be a different book if I wrote it now ... I might change Jud and Billy's mum. I feel I was a bit hard on them.'

And, speaking of change, has writing *Kes* changed his life? 'Maybe it would have if I'd written a blockbuster – one that made me lots of money. But they're so often written badly, and I couldn't do that. I write about what I believe in, and I write as well as I can.' *Kes* wasn't Barry Hines's first novel, so its success didn't change the direction of his career, but it gave him a sense of success – and of constant wonder that what he wrote as adult fiction is now an exam set text in schools and colleges.

What of the future? At the moment, having just spent two years as writer-in-residence at Sheffield Polytechnic, he's preparing a series of five plays for the BBC. Pages of the manuscript – inspired by his attending a rock concert in Sheffield – lie on his desk. 'It'll be finished by the end of the summer.'

He admits to finding writing hard work, and to occasional panics that he's dried up. 'I go over to the shelf, take down the books I've written and leaf through them, muttering, "You've done it before – you can do it again." ' I get the impression, though, that he enjoys his life, writing, giving readings of his own work, teaching and supporting young writers in schools and colleges. 'They don't believe that their own experience counts, and they think you've got to use long words to write properly. It's not true; everyday experience, down-to-earth language – that's what makes good writing.' I remember *Kes*, and I believe him.

Summary of the Plot

Barry Hines introduces his book with a quotation from a medieval manuscript written at a time when many people hunted with birds. A kestrel was considered the most suitable bird for a knave, a young wild boy. You can read more about hunting with birds on pp. 77–91.

It is night time, and Billy Casper and his brother Jud are asleep in the bed they share. When the alarm rings, Jud turns it off and goes back to sleep. Billy is worried in case Jud should be late for work and wakes him up again (p. 7). Annoyed at this, Jud thumps Billy viciously in the kidneys, then, when he himself gets up, Jud pulls all the bedclothes off Billy (p. 8). When Jud has gone, Billy goes back to sleep again (p. 9).

It is still dark when Billy gets up. He expertly lays the fire. Once again, there is nothing left for breakfast (p. 9) and Jud has taken Billy's bike to get to work. Billy walks across the estate to the newspaper shop where he does the morning paper-round (p. 10). When the owner, Mr Porter, realizes that Billy will have to walk the round, he threatens to give the lad's job to someone else (p. 11). Casually, while Porter is serving a customer, Billy steals some chocolate. Then, with a few last words, he leaves the shop (p. 12). His walk takes him up into the countryside to some rich houses. He watches a thrush catch a worm, steals some eggs and orange juice (p. 13), and then stops to read a comic from his bag (p. 15) before continuing his round (p. 16).

Back at the shop, Porter accuses Billy of not delivering the papers (p. 16) and, in retaliation, the lad tips Porter's ladder so that he loses his balance (p. 17).

Billy heads back home, just in time to see yet another of his mother's boyfriends leaving. His mother is getting ready to go to work (p. 18). She has run out of cigarettes and tries to wheedle Billy into going to the shops for her. When the lad refuses, she gets angry and tries to hit him. The two fence round each other (p. 19) and Billy runs out of the house to the sound of his mother's threats. He retaliates by throwing the eggs he has stolen at the house (p. 20). His mother goes off to work with a final threat to Billy and a reminder to him to take Jud's bet to the betting shop (p. 21).

Now his mother has gone, Billy walks to the garden shed. There he keeps a kestrel, a beautiful bird of prey. Billy talks to her affectionately and gradually starts to reminisce about the day he found her.

That particular day, a Saturday, Billy got up early to go nesting with his friends. Jud was setting off for work and chased Billy when Billy tried to eat his packed lunch (p. 22). Billy found that his friends had not yet woken up (p. 23), so he went off on his own, out into the early-morning countryside to find nests (pp. 24–5). He climbed one tree, but to his disgust the nest at the top was empty (pp. 26–7).

After that, Billy passed Monastery Farm, and, as he did so, happened to see a female kestrel on the wing (p. 27). Fascinated, the boy watched as the kestrel's mate appeared, caught its prey and passed it back to the female to take to the nest (p. 28). Billy realized that the nest was in the monastery wall, but as he went to take a closer look a farmer stopped him (p. 29). In the end, seeing the boy's interest, the farmer allowed him nearer but warned him not to interfere with the nest (pp. 30–31).

Billy's interest in the birds had been aroused. He wondered if he could take one of the kestrel chicks and rear it (p. 31). He needed to know how to do this. As a first step he tried to borrow a book on falconry from the library. He met with a frosty reception and gave up (pp. 32–3). In desperation, he stole *A Falconer's Handbook* from the local bookshop (p. 34).

Back home, Billy met with mockery from Jud (p. 35), who first questioned, then bullied him to find out more about the hawk (p. 36). In the end, however, Jud lost interest. Billy's mum, getting ready to go out on Saturday night, paid Billy hardly any attention either (p. 37). She was far too worried about leaving on time.

Later that night, Billy was in bed and still reading his book on falconry when Jud returned from a Saturday night's drinking (p. 40). Too drunk to get undressed, he made Billy help him. Disgusted, Billy did so (p. 40). Then he suddenly rebelled and started to call Jud names. Finally he hit him before fleeing out of the door (p. 41), taking his clothes with him.

Billy made his way out into the countryside, lit by the full moon (p. 41), and reached Monastery Farm safely (p. 42). He then began the difficult climb up the monastery wall. He reached the spot where the kestrel's nest was and carefully chose the strongest kestrel chick to take (p. 43). Pleased with his night's work, he set off home (p. 44).

After remembering all this, Billy suddenly comes back to the present, has a last look at Kes and then sets off for school (p. 44).

At school, the register is being called. When Mr Crossley, the form master, reaches the name Fisher, Billy automatically responds by calling out 'German Bight' (see p. 44). Angry that he has been misled into marking Fisher present, Crossley tells Billy off (p. 44), much to the amusement of the rest of the class, and then sends them all out to assembly (p. 45).

Assembly is held by the headmaster, Mr Gryce. He is a bully who orders the boys to stop coughing before the hymn (p. 46), and who demands a scapegoat when someone still coughs. He orders the whole school to sing the hymn happily (p. 47). When the Bible reading is followed by a singing of the Lord's Prayer, Billy slips off into another daydream (p. 48).

Billy's mind goes back to one of the times he took Kes out. The kestrel became frightened (p. 49), but Billy reassured her and then began to walk out into the estate with her. He attracted admiring glances, and one little boy spoke to Billy and then tried to touch the hawk, which struck out at him (pp. 50–51).

Billy is lost in his memories and is unaware that all the other boys have sat down. He is instructed to report to Gryce's room after assembly for his punishment (p. 52). When he does so, he and another boy, MacDowell, begin to argue (p. 53). Then Gryce appears, tells off the various culprits of the morning (pp. 55–6), including one boy who has just come to deliver a message (p. 54), and then orders them all to empty their pockets. The messenger is discovered to have everyone else's smoking gear in his pockets (p. 57), and so is punished along with the rest (p. 58).

When Billy returns to class, it is to an English lesson held by Mr Farthing, a good teacher who seems to have some concern for his pupils (p. 58). He is teaching them about fact and fiction (p. 59). He encourages one boy, Anderson, to tell the class about a funny experience when catching tadpoles (pp. 60–61). Then he turns to Billy (p. 62). Eventually, spurred on by the rest of the class (p. 63), the boy starts to explain about Kes. He describes how he keeps her and how he trained her (pp.

64–5). Billy warms to his subject so enthusiastically that Mr Farthing gets him to speak from the front of the class (p. 65). With Mr Farthing's encouragement, Billy explains carefully and accurately how to secure the kestrel to the gauntlet (p. 66), how to take her out and how to allow her to fly off a little on a leash (p. 67). Then he describes how he let her fly free for the first time, risking losing her altogether (pp. 68–9).

Billy's account is well received, and he is applauded for it (p. 70). Then Mr Farthing explains to the class what fiction is, and sets them the essay 'A Tall Story' (p. 71). The boys settle down to work (p. 72). Billy's tall story is about an ideal life at home, with his dad back, Jud gone away, lots of food and lots of attention (p. 73).

At break, Billy goes out into the school yard (p. 73). He happens to notice MacDowall who tries to bait him (p. 74). MacDowall then traps him near the boiler house and starts to insult Billy's mother, insinuating that he and Jud had different fathers (p. 75). They fight, and soon the news spreads across the playground (p. 76). Mr Farthing comes across at a run and drags them apart, sending the other boys away (p. 77). Then he questions both boys, eventually bullying MacDowall into tears to show him how Billy feels (pp. 78–9).

When MacDowall goes to clean up, Mr Farthing asks Billy what happened and the lad tells him of the bully's taunts (p. 80). Billy takes the opportunity to air some of his grievances about school (pp. 81–2) and Mr Farthing listens sympathetically. Billy explains that one of his problems is that now he has Kes, he no longer hangs around with the troublemakers, and so they have turned on him (p. 83). Mr Farthing reminds him that soon he will be leaving school. Surely his life will be better then. Billy is not optimistic, but looks forward to having money to spend on falconry (p. 84). Finally, Farthing says he wants to see Billy's kestrel, and they arrange to meet one lunchtime (p. 85).

Billy runs off to the toilets and washes. He really enjoys blowing bubbles with the soap (p. 86). Then he goes to the changing room where his class is getting ready for football (p. 86). Mr Sugden, the games master, a frustrated professional footballer, turns on him for being late. When Billy tells him that he has no kit, this is the last straw (p. 87). Sugden hits him with the ball and then drags out a huge old pair of shorts (p. 88). Billy puts them on, much to the amusement of the rest of the class (p. 89), and they all go out on to the field.

Sugden and Tibbut, a good football player, are the captains of each side, and pick their teams (p. 90). They aim to pick the best players for their teams first, and Billy is almost the last one chosen (p. 91).

Mr Sugden takes off his tracksuit to reveal full league football kit, much to the amusement of the boys (p. 92). Then Sugden notices there is no one in goal and sends Billy there. The lad protests all the way (p. 93).

The game begins (p. 94). It is obvious that Sugden is playing only for himself, with the boys as supporting cast. Billy is bored in goal. After a quarter of an hour, he lets a ball in. In revenge, Sugden throws the muddy ball at him (p. 95), then continues to play, badly (p. 96), awarding his own side a penalty to equalize (p. 97).

Billy meanwhile amuses himself by climbing up the goal netting, pretending to be a chimpanzee (p. 97). Sugden shouts at him to come down, which he does to a round of applause (p. 98). Two more goals are scored, one for each side, when a stray dog runs on to the field and takes the ball. Sugden is all set to fetch cricket bats and beat the dog off (p. 99), but Billy makes friends with it and leads it off the field.

When Billy returns, his team has pulled ahead, but he soon lets another goal in. Sugden decrees that the next goal is the winner, disallows a goal against his side (p. 100), and even when the bell goes tells the boys to play on. Everything becomes serious (p. 101). Billy desperately wants to let a goal in so he can get home to feed Kes (p. 102). Eventually, he does let in a goal and the game ends.

Billy is dressed when Sugden comes into the changing room. He stops the boy, insisting – in revenge for the lost game – that Billy should take a shower (p. 103).

In the end Billy gives in, undresses and hurries into the hot showers (p. 105). As he runs through to the other end, Sugden blocks him and motions three of the boys to stop Billy's exit the other way. Then he turns the shower to cold (p. 106). Billy yells, tries to escape, then finally stands still in silence (p. 107). The class's sympathy is now with Billy. Sugden refuses to let him out, but when the lad climbs over the partition and out of the showers, he is allowed to go (p. 108).

Back home, Billy hurries to see Kes. He then decides to shoot some meat for her. He fetches the air rifle from the house, noticing on the way that Jud has left some money to be placed as a bet (p. 109). Billy eventually takes the money to place the bet for Jud. Then he goes to the garage and waits for sparrows to alight (p. 110). He easily and quickly sights one and shoots it (p. 111), then retrieves it and puts it, with his other gear, into a satchel.

He goes to fetch Kes, takes her on to the gauntlet, and then carries her out to the field. She flies free. Then Billy urges her with the lure to come to him. At that moment Mr Farthing arrives. Billy tells him not to come too close (p. 112). Then he continues casting Kes off and luring her back (pp. 113–14). When he has finished, Farthing congratulates him, then watches while Kes devours the sparrow Billy has shot for her (p. 115).

They go back to the shed and, once Billy has settled the bird, he and Mr Farthing talk (p. 116). Billy reveals that he has kept many animals. But the hawk is special, particularly when it flies. It looks so beautifully proportioned (p. 117). Billy and Mr Farthing seem to share the same feelings about the bird. They both respect its wildness, the fact that it is not a pet (p. 118).

It is late. Mr Farthing has to get back to school (p. 119). Billy refuses his offer of a lift, and the teacher leaves. Left alone, Billy picks up the kestrel's pellet and crumbles it (p. 120), finding inside the remains of the tiny animal Kes has eaten. He plays with the pieces and finally grinds them into the ground before leaving the hut.

Billy next goes to the betting shop (p. 121). On the way, however, he is drawn by the smell from the fish and chip shop and has to decide whether to take Jud's money and buy himself some food or place Jud's bet. He tosses a coin to help him decide, and this results in his going to place the bet (pp. 122–3). But when the bookie tells him the horses have not much chance of winning, Billy decides to risk Jud's anger and spend the money instead (p. 124). He goes into Hartley's, buys a small amount of fish and chips and some scraps (p. 125), then spends the rest of the money on beef for Kes and on cigarettes (p. 126). Then he goes back to school.

The afternoon has turned stormy (p. 126). Billy is back at school, doing maths. He is so weary he starts to fall asleep. As he is staring out of the window, he thinks he sees Jud walking into the school (p. 127).

Then Jud walks down the corridor, looks in, walks on, stops, turns back and looks in again. Billy is terrified and starts to cry (p. 128). When the lesson finishes, his only escape is to walk out of the classroom with the teacher, with Jud following them (p. 129).

Billy runs into the toilets and out of the side door. Jud follows him in, banging each of the cubicle doors in turn. But Billy has escaped, first into the cloakrooms (p. 130), then on to the cycle shed and the boiler room (p. 131), where he nods off in the warmth. When he wakes up he finds himself locked in, but he easily undoes the lock, and runs back into the school (p. 132). He rushes about looking for his classmates (p. 133) and when at last he finds them he realizes he has missed his Youth Employment interview. Gryce tells him off again (p. 134), then sends him to the medical room for the interview.

Waiting to see the Youth Employment Officer (p. 135), Billy overhears another boy being nagged by his mother to try for an office job. When they go in, Billy is left alone, studying the linoleum, the fire alarm, his own feet (p. 136). In a while, it is his turn. The Youth Employment Officer calls him in, getting his name wrong and so beginning the whole interview in an awkward fashion (p. 137). He asks Billy about his abilities and the sorts of things he wants to do. When Billy finds difficulty in answering (p. 138), the officer delivers a lecture on employment and study – all of which means nothing to Billy. Getting no response from Billy the officer suggests he goes down the mine – but Billy refuses point-blank. Frustrated the man asks about Billy's hobbies. Has he any? (p. 139).

Remembering Kes, and now struck by a sudden fear, Billy quickly asks if he can go. He rushes out of school and runs all the way home. When he gets there, he finds the shed broken into and Kes gone (p. 140).

Billy calls Kes's name, then dashes into the house, searching each room to find Jud. When he finds no one he runs out on to the field, the lure in his hand, calling for Kes again (p. 141).

Then he runs to the betting shop where the bookie's wife tells him that Jud turned up to claim his winnings. Both horses won and Jud should have got ten pounds. He was furiously angry and at first would not believe that Billy had not placed the bet. Now Jud is going to take revenge (p. 142).

Billy runs back to the fields, working the lure and calling in the hope that Kes will come back to him (p. 143). Then he crosses a stile and goes on towards the woods, breaking the lure line as he does so, but still calling (p. 144). Then the rain begins hurtling down, as Billy runs and calls (p. 145). He gets soaked through. Dusk gathers as he reaches Monastery Farm where he stops for a while, remembering when he found Kes. Then he turns back to the estate, collecting the broken lure line on the way (p. 146).

When Billy bursts into the house, Jud and his mother are both there. He faces Jud, ignoring his mother's attempts to divert him (p. 147). Jud, dipping biscuits in tea, shouts at Billy, who rushes at him, and they begin to fight. His mother wonders what the matter is, and Jud explains that Billy failed to put the bet on so Jud has lost ten pounds (p. 148). In return, Billy blurts out that Jud has killed his hawk. When Jud admits it, the boy runs to his mother for comfort, but she does not respond to him (p. 149). Billy then rushes at Jud, swearing at him. Jud finally admits that the hawk is in the dustbin.

Billy goes and retrieves the body, gently stroking it, then bringing it back into the house (p. 150). Faced with the evidence, his mother recoils but does remonstrate with Jud. Billy urges her to punish Jud, but she knows she cannot. With total lack of understanding, she suggests to Billy that '. . . it's only a bird. You can get another . . .' (p. 151).

Billy hits out at his mother, sending her tea flying (p. 151), and then attacks Jud. In a final gesture he swings the hawk at them before turning to run out of the house. His mother calls after him, the neighbours all gather at their gates to watch, but Billy has gone (p. 152).

Billy runs, then walks, still carrying the body of the hawk with him. He makes his way round and round the estate (p. 154), passing his friends' houses, walking down City Road, past Porter's shop (p. 155). Eventually he comes to an old, derelict cinema. He finds his way in through a small boarded-up window (pp. 156–7) and sees he is in an old toilet. He lights his way with matches and newspaper into the foyer and then into the auditorium.

Billy walks down to the front, then back again, pulls out an old cushion, lets his newspaper torch die away and then sits in the darkness.

Memories come to him, memories of a happier time when he used to come to the cinema with his dad, as a very little boy. Billy remembers being in the cinema, eating ice cream, feeling happy (p. 158). These memories are like the separate pictures, or 'stills', that make up a film. Then he remembers coming home with his dad, finding a family friend in the house with his mum, seeing his dad hit the man. The next thing Billy remembers is being in bed, hearing shouting, and seeing his dad leaving, suitcase packed.

Billy's mind drifts away from these old, unhappy memories, and suddenly it is as if he is in the picture on a cinema screen. He is with Kes, and they are both the heroes of the film, admired by the audience. They are on the moor, and instead of a sparrow or a mouse, it is Jud who is Kes's prey, whom Kes follows, on whom Kes swoops (p. 159). But in the end Kes does not catch Jud. Jud wins, and Kes and Billy lose.

Billy rushes out of the cinema, suddenly feeling bad about the place. After a while he goes home. He has nothing left to do but to bury the hawk and go to bed.

Commentary

The quotation at the start of the book says that a kestrel is the right bird for a knave – a young, wild boy. Who do you think the knave is in this book? Barry Hines originally called his work *A Kestrel for a Knave* – the film title *Kes* has become so popular that it has now been adopted as the name of the book.

SECTION 1, pp. 7–9

In this section we first meet Billy, and Jud his brother. They are lying in bed, probably in the early hours of the morning, just before Jud has to get up to go to work at the pit.

At once we learn something about the way they live. How do you know immediately that the family is poor – what clues can you find throughout the scene to back this up?

The first section of any book is important because the writer has to catch your interest immediately. Barry Hines tries to do this by choosing a scene most of us know – waking up in the morning – and making it interesting by having something violent happen. Does this in fact catch your interest? Think about this. You might explain to someone else why you did (or didn't) find this section interesting or exciting.

Another use for an introductory section is to show you, the reader, what some of the main characters are like. Read the section again, this time thinking about the people involved, Billy and Jud. This is the first time we have met them, but already, in two and a half pages, we know quite a lot about them. As you read, jot down what you notice about each of them – collect five words to describe each character.

When you have done this, you will probably have realized that Jud is bigger and stronger than Billy (he is his big brother), he bullies him, he is violent, he is selfish. Billy actually does think about Jud – look at how he wakes him up and he doesn't fight back, though he argues. Keep the notes you have made, because both Billy and Jud are important characters in the book and you will need to think more about them later.

SECTION 2, pp. 9–16

Next, we see Billy getting up. We see again – from the lack of food in the larder, the fact he puts his mum's sweater on – that the family are not well off.

Barry Hines also spends nearly a page describing to us how Billy lays the fire and gets it going. You may never have had to lay and light a fire, so read that paragraph once or twice to get a clear idea in your mind of what Billy does. Why do you think Barry Hines goes to so much trouble to describe all this – what might he be trying to show us about Billy?

Jud has taken Billy's bike to get to work – another example of his bullying – so Billy walks to the newsagent's to do his paper-round. There is a very clear account of how he does this, describing things he sees and hears, the people he passes. Make a list of what Billy sees and hears. Then think back to the last time you walked somewhere in the early morning. What did you see and hear? Were they the same sort of things as Billy – or do you live somewhere completely different?

When Billy arrives at the shop, it is obvious that he does not get on well with the owner. We will look later at the relationship between them, but, for the moment, see if you can find three things that Porter does or says that are unfair to Billy, and then notice how Billy takes his revenge. Should he have done it? What is so funny about Billy's comment a few lines further on (p. 12) that 'I've stopped getting into trouble now'?

When he leaves the shop, Billy starts off on his round. He has to walk it all, so it can't be easy. If you have ever done a paper-round (or collected house-to-house), notice if any of the things Billy sees are familiar to you. Has Barry Hines mentioned any details that seem to you absolutely right? Or absolutely wrong? Notice particularly the thrush Billy sees.

Most of the houses Billy calls at are richer than his. How do we know this? Read through the section again and see if you can work out what Billy's attitude might be to these houses and the people who live in them. Look particularly at the way he looks through the letter-box of the stone house.

During the round, Billy also meets the milkman. They chat to each other. Billy seems friendly, if a little critical of the horse – but he also steals some eggs and some orange juice. We know already that he has been in trouble before, probably for stealing, and he doesn't seem to have broken the habit. Do you blame Billy for stealing the eggs and the juice? And what else has he already stolen? Think whether there is any difference between Billy's stealing from Porter and from the milkman. Does the fact that he doesn't get caught alter what you feel about Billy's stealing?

After meeting the milkman, Billy stops to read a page from the *Dandy* – he obviously likes Desperate Dan, for he turns to that page at once. Read the account of the cartoon. Is it funny? What does it tell you about Billy?

By this time, you should have a fairly good idea of what Billy is like as a person. Write down some words that you think describe him (you might like to use the notes you collected for Section 1) and then write a paragraph about Billy, including the most important things you want to say about him.

SECTION 3, pp. 16–21

Back at the shop, Porter immediately turns on Billy again, suspecting him of dumping the papers and trespassing. Read again the section on pages 11 and 12, then this section, pages 16 and 17. Think about the way Billy and Porter behave to each other. Porter goes on at Billy, but Billy gets his revenge by stealing and by rocking the ladder so that Porter loses his balance. So is Porter right in suspecting Billy all the time? And is Billy right to take his revenge? Imagine you are Porter, and write down three things you might say in an argument to prove yourself right. Then imagine you are Billy and do the same. Decide who seems to you to be right in the end.

After this, Billy goes home. This is the first time we see him with his mum. What sort of person is she? Do as you did earlier for Billy; read through this section and jot down five words that tell you what Billy's mum is like. Then use these words to write a description of her. Do you think that if you met Billy's mum you would like her?

Billy and his mum have an argument. She wants him to go to the shops and buy her cigarettes. He is worried, for two reasons. First, he doesn't want to be late for school. Secondly, he knows his mum owes the shop money. What do you think Billy is afraid will happen when he goes to the shop?

The argument between Billy and his mum is quite a vicious one, and has a number of stages. This is a list of some of the things that happen during the argument: put them in the correct order.

1. Billy's mum falls on the floor.
2. Billy's mum offers him money to go to the shop.
3. Billy makes a pretend move and his mother dives at him.
4. Billy says the shop won't be open.
5. Billy says the shop won't give him any more credit.
6. Billy and his mum chase each other round the table.
7. Billy's mum finds she has no cigarettes.
8. Billy says he will be late for school if he goes to the shop.
9. Billy's mum asks Billy to go to the shops for her.
10. Billy says he'll be punished if he's late for school.
11. Billy's mum tries to hit him.
12. Billy runs out of the house.

Think back to an argument or disagreement you may have had with someone, possibly one of your parents. Where were you? What could you see, hear, feel? In what order did things happen? Write a short account of the argument, making sure you start at the beginning and finish at the end. Notice any differences between the argument you had and the one Billy had with his mum. Notice any similarities.

How do you think Billy felt after he ran out of the kitchen? He certainly chooses a dramatic way to get his own back – throwing eggs at the house. Then his mum comes out on her way to work. She has a parting shot for Billy – a reminder to take Jud's betting slip to the shop and put a bet on. (Why can't Jud do this himself?) This betting slip is important later on – if you have read the whole book already, see if you can remember why.

Once Billy's mum has gone, he does not go straight to school. Instead, he walks down to the shed at the end of the garden, where he keeps his kestrel. This point in the book is vital. It is the first time we see Billy with Kes, the bird that is so important to him. Read the section on page 21 from 'When he heard the gate bang . . .' to '. . . The hawk watched it all the time.' What can you tell immediately about Billy's feelings for Kes? Look particularly at the description of the shed, the description of the bird, the way Billy talks to her. It is as if Kes is a person, a friend he can trust.

One of the main points in the story of *Kes* is that Billy's relationship with the kestrel is different from the relationships he has in the rest of his life. Start thinking about this now. What does he feel about Kes that he does not feel about anyone else? Think back over the people in Billy's life you've read about so far. List them (there are four). Are there any of them you think Billy ought to prefer to the kestrel?

At the end of this section, Billy is talking to Kes, and begins to reminisce about the day he first got her. This is the signal for a 'flashback', a section in the book where we step out of present time and back into the past.

SECTION 4, pp. 21–32

The day Billy first finds Kes is a Saturday. He gets up early, but Jud is already up and having breakfast. Where is he going? Jud teases Billy by telling him that next year he will be going there too. This is one of the times in the book when Billy stands up for himself with Jud. Why is he so definite? What job do you think Billy might want to do instead? Why is Jud particularly cruel to tease him about it?

When Jud leaves, Billy calmly unwraps his brother's packed lunch ('snap') and begins to eat it. Of course, when Jud returns he goes for Billy. This is yet another example of the rows the two have in the book. Whose fault do you think it is this time?

Billy runs away from Jud and carries on to his friends' houses. They have agreed to go bird nesting together, so he tries to wake them up by throwing earth and pebbles at their windows. There is no answer from Tibby, and at MacDowall's house his mother answers, and tells Billy off. In revenge, he throws a last handful of pebbles at the glass before running away.

In the course of the book, we see Billy several times with other boys of his age. How do they react to him? Do they like him? Here, he has got up early because MacDowall suggested going bird nesting – but neither of the other two boys has bothered. What does this tell you about Tibby and MacDowall? You might also like to wonder why Billy is keen to go nesting when the other two are not. Are they interested in different things? At this point in the book, Billy and MacDowall are friends. What happens later on? Why do they split up? Turn to page 83 for help on this, if you need to.

Billy decides to go nesting by himself. He leaves the estate and walks through the countryside, through fields full of flowers, and through the woods. Read the description of his walk from page 24 to the point where he leans against the beech tree on page 26. Write down six things Billy sees, six things he hears and six things he touches.

Think about a walk you have taken, in either the countryside or the town. Write down six things you have seen, six you have heard, six you might touch. Now write a paragraph, describing one part of the walk you remember particularly clearly.

It is obvious from the way Billy behaves when he is in the country that nature is very important to him. He loves the dew on the grass. He is very gentle with the baby thrushes. When he finds a tree that he thinks might have a nest in it, though, he is not worried about climbing the tree and trying to steal the eggs. Imagine you found Billy stealing eggs. Write down some things you might say to him to explain why taking eggs from nests is not a good idea. What reasons might Billy give you for doing so?

In fact Billy only finds an empty nest, full of old leaves and twigs, and so he carries on walking through the woods. As he nears Monastery Farm a kestrel flies out from a hole in the monastery wall. Notice how quickly Billy kneels, then lies down, so that he won't be noticed and can watch the kestrel. He is fascinated by it – by its movements, by the way it waits for its mate.

The male kestrel hovers, drops, hovers again, then stoops to take its prey. The way this is described – carefully, accurately, using words like 'breath-taking' – shows us how impressed Billy is by the kestrel. The prey is transferred from one bird to the other, and the female takes it back to the nest. At this point, Billy obviously has some very clear thoughts in his head. Write down three or four sentences to explain what you guess Billy is thinking and feeling at this time.

Billy dozes for a while, and it is almost midday when he makes his way over to the farm. He wants to explore the monastery wall. But before he can do so, the farmer's little girl spots him and the farmer comes out.

What sort of experience do you think the farmer has had with kids from the estate? What do you think he is feeling when he first speaks to Billy? Billy answers him directly and persistently, but at first the farmer says there isn't a nest there. Why? He is also worried in case Billy tries to climb the wall and hurts himself.

In the end the farmer admits to Billy that he and his family know all about the nest. Why do you think he starts to sympathize with Billy? What does Billy say, and what feelings does he show that make the farmer smile and talk to him?

It is when Billy says confidently that he would like to train a young kestrel that the farmer gets worried. He asks Billy how he would do it, then says, 'That's why I won't let anybody near, 'cos if they can't be kept properly it's criminal' (p. 31). What does he mean by this? He warns Billy that kestrels are not easy to train and that he has never known anyone who could do it. Later in the book, Billy trains a kestrel. What does this show about him?

Read back from the point on page 29 where Billy first meets the farmer to the point on page 32 where he runs off. Then imagine that you are the farmer, telling his wife that lunchtime all about meeting Billy. Start off: 'There was a young lad up near the monastery wall this morning...' Say what Billy was like, the things you talked about, the impression you got of Billy – and a few of your fears.

SECTION 5, pp. 32–9

Billy isn't clever. He can hardly read and write. But in this section of the book we see that he can get over this if he wants to do something. He first goes to the library. Read pages 32 to 33, where Billy speaks to the girl in the library, then write down five words to describe her. Do you like her? Why? Or why not? Why do you think she acts as she does?

Billy is not allowed to read about falconry in the library, but in the end he does get a book. How? Do you think Billy is wrong to do this? Whose responsibility do you think it is that he is able to do so – Billy's, his mother's, the girl in the library's responsibility? Is anyone else to blame?

When Billy gets home, he settles down to try to read the book. For someone who 'can't read' he gets a long way. But, as always, he has no peace. Jud immediately snatches the book, and teases and bullies Billy about it. It would have been better if Jud had encouraged Billy, but instead he puts him down. Notice that Jud doesn't tell Billy off for stealing, but rather for stealing books instead of money. Notice, too, how Billy protects the book – smoothing the covers, defending it, proudly saying he is going to train a kestrel. He doesn't want to tell Jud where he is going to get a kestrel to train, in case Jud shoots the young birds. How realistic is this fear?

There are lots of differences between Billy and Jud. If you read this whole incident carefully, you might notice at least half a dozen. Write them down. Think particularly about the two boys' interests, attitudes, personalities. When the word 'bird' is mentioned, what does each boy think of? Notice that at this point Billy has definitely decided to train a kestrel. When do you think he made up his mind?

Next, Billy's mum comes in. Like Jud, she is getting ready to go out for the evening. This is far more important to her than Billy's interests – or even whether he is going to get any tea that night. Find some examples of things Billy's mum says or does that show us how uninterested she is in Billy. Write them down on one side of the page. On the other side of the page, write down what Billy's mum could have said or done if she really cared for him.

What is Billy's mum's relationship with Jud? Look at the section where they talk about the evening. What do you learn from this about the two of them? Like previous scenes, we also get clues here that Billy's family is poor. How many clues can you find?

Left alone, Billy carries on reading his book, with difficulty.

SECTION 6, pp. 39–41

During the evening, Billy goes to bed but carries on reading *A Falconer's Handbook* until he hears someone coming home.

It is Jud, drunk after his evening out. He speaks to Billy, who pretends to be asleep, then tries to undress but can't get out of his trousers. Jud flops down on the bed, forcing Billy to undress him, grumbling all the time.

Jud seems to come home drunk regularly. How do we know? He is really pretty revolting when he is drunk. Make a list of the things he does and says that tell us how drunk he is.

Suddenly, Billy has had enough. With Jud helpless, he can have his revenge. So he holds Jud's mouth closed so that he can't breathe. Then he claws at him, chanting insults as he stamps round the bed, and finally, on the last word, hits him.

Billy reacts more violently than ever before. Why do you think this is? It is certainly to do with the fact that Jud is now helpless and Billy has power over him. What do you learn about Billy from the way he reacts? What sort of person do you now think he is?

When he hits Jud, Billy runs for his life, but as he reaches the kitchen door he realizes that Jud has gone to sleep again, and so he is safe. He takes his time dressing before he leaves the house. He is going to get a kestrel.

SECTION 7, pp. 41–4

As Billy sets off, it is a moonlit night. He walks through the dark wood, which seems like a street full of houses. Then he hears an owl call.

Expertly he answers it, and calls to the owl during the whole of his walk to the farmhouse. What does this tell us about Billy?

All is quiet at the farmhouse. Billy already knows the climb up the monastery wall is dangerous, but he still wants to do it. He does it well, carefully. He does not disturb the bird, or anyone at the farmhouse.

When Billy reaches the place where he believes the nest is, he feels into the hole and finds the young birds. How does he decide which one he is going to take?

When Billy has finished choosing – notice how gently and carefully he does it – he puts the best bird into his pocket and, carefully supporting it, makes his way home.

Imagine you are Billy at school on Monday morning. Your friends Tibby and MacDowall, who let you down over nesting, have asked you how you spent the weekend. Tell them about your adventure on Saturday night from the point where you reached the wall, all about getting the birds, and ending when you are walking home. You really want them to understand not only what you did, but how you felt about it – scared, excited, triumphant. Write down what you would say.

You might like to wonder how Billy spent his Sunday, having a young kestrel to look after. He had already built a nesting box. What else would he have to do for the young hawk? Would it be easy? What might he feel? How did Jud and Billy's mum react?

SECTION 8, pp. 44–6

Back in the present, Billy has left the hawk and has gone to school. He is in class while the register is being called. Almost all the scenes in the book set in school show the place as being cruel, unsympathetic and unhelpful to Billy. Here, as Mr Crossley, Billy's form master, reads out the register, Billy first answers to his own name. Then he hears the name Fisher. This is both the name of one of the boys in Billy's class and also of one of the parts into which weathermen divide the North Sea. In weather forecasts, the name 'German Bight' follows 'Fisher' and so Billy calls this out. This confuses Crossley and he begins to mark an absent pupil as present. He is furious, and turns on Billy.

Read this scene through, then pick out from the following list four words or phrases you could use to describe Crossley. Use them to write a few lines about him.

helpful	kind
sarcastic	bullying
supportive	soft-hearted
a good educationalist	a disciplinarian
timid	reticent
unsympathetic	compassionate

It is not only Billy's teacher who fails to understand the way his mind works. His classmates don't seem very understanding either. How do they behave towards Billy? What do they say to him, and how do they react when he speaks? Find out the meaning of the word 'scapegoat'. Do you think this word describes Billy?

SECTION 9, pp. 46–8

From Billy's classroom, the scene changes to school assembly. The headmaster, Gryce, is a tyrant. He dominates the school, and we see him here in assembly stopping the boys from coughing, trying to speed up the singing, threatening the boys, bullying them.

An assembly is meant to be a time when a school gathers together, in this case to pray and hear announcements. Mr Gryce seems to say that the assembly should be happy. Look at the title of the hymn: he calls it 'a hymn of joy'. But this assembly is anything but happy. What words and actions particularly of Gryce's – but also of Crossley's – make it a horrible and frightening experience for the boys?

Look at the Bible reading on page 48. Barry Hines has chosen this passage deliberately. Though it is about sheep, Christ actually meant that even one person who is 'lost' – that is, who gets into trouble or is unhappy – matters to God, particularly if that person is small and helpless. Who might this one small, helpless person be in *Kes*?

SECTION 10, pp. 48–51

While everyone is singing the Lord's Prayer, Billy daydreams again, this time about the more recent past, to a day when Kes has grown into an adult hawk.

Billy is taking her out, and to do so, he has to fasten her firmly to him. Here is a list of the things Billy does. Put them in the right order. It might help you to look up these words in the glossary first: gauntlet, swivel, jesses, leash.

1. Kes steps onto the gauntlet and Billy lets her stay there.
2. Billy distracts Kes by moving the meat.
3. Billy loops the leash around his glove and ties the end.
4. Kes eats her meat and behaves as Billy walks her round the garden.
5. Billy approaches Kes with a piece of meat in the gauntlet.
6. While Kes eats the meat, Billy threads a leash through the swivel.
7. Billy takes Kes out into the garden.
8. Kes steps onto the gauntlet, but Billy replaces her on the perch.
9. Kes throws herself off the glove and Billy lifts her back.
10. Billy attaches a swivel to the jesses on Kes's legs.

Billy attracts lots of attention as he walks round the estate with Kes. What do you think people say to each other about him? In particular, one small child cycles up and questions Billy. Read the section where Billy talks to the kid while the child tries to stroke Kes. Billy is not behaving as he does in school. How does he react? What does having Kes give him that he doesn't have when he is on his own?

SECTION 11, pp. 51–3

Billy is so busy with his memories that he does not notice that the Lord's Prayer is over and the boys around him have sat down. Gryce makes Billy stand while he tells him off, then orders the boy to come to his office later for a caning. Here we see the sort of treatment Billy gets at school, and we also learn more about the sort of pupil he is. He is known as a troublemaker.

Gryce reads the final announcements at assembly. Notice the one about appointments with the Youth Employment Officer. It is particularly important, for Billy has to attend an interview with the officer. If you have read the book through, you may remember why Billy is late for his appointment. Read this section and pages 46 to 48 about assembly, then think back to a school assembly you have attended. Remember what you could see and hear, the atmosphere, and how you felt. Was it like the assembly described in the book or was it very different? Write about it.

SECTION 12, pp. 53–8

Billy goes to wait with MacDowall, and three boys caught for smoking, in Gryce's office. MacDowall immediately begins to tease Billy. They have fallen out, you may remember, because Billy spends so much time with Kes. Billy faces up to MacDowall at once. He is not a coward.

A messenger comes to Gryce's door, and is bullied into hiding the cigarettes and lighters belonging to the three smokers. When Gryce arrives he sends all the boys into his office, but does not give the innocent messenger time to explain that he has nothing to do with the smokers. Gryce then delivers a two-page lecture to the boys.

Read this section again. It shows us a great deal about Gryce. How does he feel about the school, about young people, about today's generation? How do you think a headmaster should feel about the pupils he works with? Does Gryce feel like this?

Imagine Gryce is applying for another job, as head of a large comprehensive school. You have been asked to write your honest opinion of whether he would be suitable for the job. What would you write?

After his speech, Gryce makes all the boys empty their pockets. The messenger tries to escape by telling Gryce what he was sent for, but Gryce will not listen to him. Then, when he finds the smoking equipment in the messenger's pockets, he decides to cane him too. Later in the book (p. 81), Billy complains about this. You might like to think, though, whether the messenger was to blame for hiding the smoking equipment in the first place. Did he have any choice?

Why do you think Barry Hines tells us about the caning? Use the following questions to help you. What does the caning tell us about Gryce? How are we meant to feel about the school and what goes on there? How does it add to our idea of Billy's life as a hard one? What does it tell us about Billy?

Even if you have never been to a school which used corporal punishment, you may feel very strongly about it. Write down three reasons why pupils should be punished by being hit. Then write down three reasons why not. Use these six sentences to write a conversation between two teachers in a staffroom, or two pupils on the way home, arguing about whether or not corporal punishment should be used.

SECTION 13, pp. 58–73

Billy goes back to class, in time for an English lesson. The teacher is Mr Farthing. From the beginning he seems sympathetic towards Billy. Mr Farthing is the only person in the book who shows Billy any understanding or sympathy, so he is important.

Mr Farthing is teaching the boys about the difference between fact and fiction. He explains, asks for examples, and encourages Anderson and Billy to give factual accounts. Then he asks the boys to write a fictional 'tall story'. Read about the lesson, then ask yourself whether or not it is a good way to teach.

Next look at Mr Farthing himself, the way he behaves and how he treats the boys. He has control over them, and doesn't let them slack. When he sets them the essay, they work and keep at it until the end of the lesson. Mr Farthing does not allow any cheek or insolence either. He is very firm with Billy when the boy will not reply to his questions.

The class seem to react to him well, though. They understand the points he is making. They respect him for not allowing any bad behaviour, and because of Mr Farthing they listen when Anderson and Billy are talking.

Apart from this, Mr Farthing really seems interested in what the boys are doing. Read again the section where he gets Billy talking and pick out three things Mr Farthing does to encourage the boy. How does this differ from the way Billy is treated by Gryce, Crossley and (later) Sugden?

Can you find any time in the lesson when Farthing does lose his temper? Notice particularly his threat to keep the whole class in after school. Is this fair?

Earlier, we suggested that you should imagine that Gryce was applying for a job as headmaster of a new school, and asked you to write a report on whether you thought he was suitable. This new school also needs a senior English teacher. Would you recommend Farthing? Why – or why not?

This particular section of the book also shows us a lot more about Billy. We have already seen him enthusiastically catching and feeding his hawk, but we have never heard him talk about it. At first, he is unsure. What do you think he is afraid of? He exchanges words with Tibby. Then, with Mr Farthing's questioning, he starts to get into the subject. Billy really is an expert, as Farthing comments later. He knows what he is talking about and he loves the hawk.

Billy is also very different here from the way he appears in other parts of the book. Divide this list of comments into two, one half describing Billy as he seems when he is talking about Kes, the other describing him as he appears normally.

1. 'an expert'
2. 'he can't read or write'
3. 'he loves that hawk'
4. 'he'll never amount to much'
5. 'he's a little thief'
6. 'he knows what he's doing, that lad'
7. 'isn't interested in anything'
8. 'he's taken the trouble to learn all about it – he's even read books'
9. 'he's confident and sure of himself'
10. 'class comic – round the bend'

Notice how the class reacts to Billy after he has spoken – a round of applause, rather than laughter. It is possible that Billy might have gained enough respect in the class from that one lesson to help him improve in other ways. (But what happens to prevent that?)

One of the really good things about Billy's speech is that he describes how to train a hawk and at the same time lets us feel the emotion behind what he has been doing. If someone asked you how Billy felt while he was training the hawk, what would you say? Think particularly of how he felt when he let Kes go free for the first time.

Don't forget, when reading this section, that Anderson's story is there too. Why do you think Barry Hines included it? Is it as good as Billy's story?

Finally, before the lesson finishes, Mr Farthing tells the boys to write 'A Tall Story'. Billy obviously thinks that the most unlikely thing that could happen to him would be to have life just the way he wants it. Read Billy's tall story, and write down at least eight things he wants to happen. It is sad that Billy's life is so far removed from what he wants. If his family life had been the way he imagines it, what sort of boy might Billy have been? Would he have trained Kes?

SECTION 14, pp. 73–85

This section begins with a description of the school playground. Is it anything like any school playground you have known? What are the differences and similarities?

The first main incident in the section is Billy's fight with MacDowall. They snap at each other, then MacDowall begins to pick on Billy until Billy can stand no more and goes for MacDowall. The way MacDowall picks on Billy shows us clearly what sort of lad he is. Look back at previous occasions in the book when we met him, and then write down ten words to describe him.

From outside, Billy seems just as bad as MacDowall – he too misbehaved at assembly, was caned, and is now in trouble again. He fights back with words and actions. But is Billy as bad as MacDowall? Is he a bully? Does he stir up trouble? Why is it that we feel more sympathy for Billy than we do for MacDowall?

The fight itself is well described. Notice the way in which the two lads tackle each other and the reaction of the other boys. If you have ever been at a playground fight, or if you can imagine one, jot down some words to remind yourself of what you saw, heard and felt while it was happening. Then write about it so that anyone who reads what you have written could really picture the fight.

Just as Billy's fight with MacDowall is in full swing, Mr Farthing arrives to stop what is happening. Was he right to do so? Were the boys right to fight in the first place? Mr Farthing sends the others away and then tackles Billy and MacDowall. At once they both start blaming each other, but Mr Farthing isn't interested in 'fault' – he is just disgusted that they are both fighting and have made such a mess.

Then MacDowall again starts threatening Billy. Farthing's reaction is interesting; he himself starts to bully MacDowall. He pushes him on the shoulder, hits him, drags him up by the lapels, all the time shouting at him, threatening him, until MacDowall, like Billy, is crying. Then Farthing tells him to go and get cleaned up, and spend the next period tidying the coke and the dustbins.

Why does Farthing do all this? Which of these reasons seem to you most likely – you can choose more than one, and you might like to discuss them with your friends.

1. Farthing has a grudge against MacDowall and is taking revenge.
2. Farthing wants to make MacDowall realize what it feels like to be bullied.
3. Farthing dislikes MacDowall.
4. Farthing has taken to Billy and wants to protect him.
5. Farthing aims to discourage MacDowall from bullying younger boys.
6. Farthing has lost his temper and is taking it out on MacDowall.
7. Farthing is a bully.

After MacDowall has disappeared, Farthing turns to Billy. He calms him down, then talks to him for a while. He really does seem interested in Billy, and allows him to talk about his problems – with school, with friends, with getting a job. Notice how Billy criticizes the school and the teachers, yet Farthing doesn't tell him off. Do you think this is a good idea?

For once Billy seems to have found an ally. The boys in his class respect him more now, and he also has a friend, an adult he can talk to, who seems concerned about him.

And Billy does talk. He says more about himself (rather than about Kes) in these pages than anywhere else in the book. Make notes about the new things we learn about Billy, his thoughts and feelings, under these headings: School; Family; Friends; Interests; Future; Ideas of himself.

Which does he say least about? Why do you think this is?

One of the most important things Billy says about himself is that 'there's allus somebody after me' (p. 83). From what you have read of the book, do you think that is true? If you were Mr Farthing, what would you say to Billy to help him keep out of trouble?

At the every end of this section, Farthing says he wants to see Billy's hawk. He is really interested in it and his visit to see Kes stoop is one of the high points of the book. Check in your own mind that you know when this is. Does Farthing see the hawk that day? At what time? Where?

Farthing blows the whistle for the end of break, while Billy goes off to wash.

SECTION 15, pp. 85–6

This section describes the school toilets, and Billy washing his hands and face, then blowing bubbles. It is a good description, showing us how Billy finds beauty in very ugly surroundings. Have you ever blown bubbles? Use five of the words in this section to describe what you saw, heard and felt when you blew bubbles.

SECTION 16, pp. 86–103

After washing, Billy goes to the changing rooms for the games lesson. Mr Sugden the games master, in his immaculate football kit, tells him off for being late and then for not having kit of his own.

Sugden is not a born teacher. He is a frustrated footballer who hasn't made the grade and so has had to teach games. As you read through this section, look out for clues to this in the way Sugden dresses, plays football, treats the boys.

At the start of the section, Sugden is just too neat to be true. He is far more concerned about his appearance than about the class he is teaching. He bullies Billy, finding him, in the end, a pair of shorts that are far too big.

This scene, in which Sugden makes Billy wear the shorts even though he is mocked by the rest of the class, is a cruel one. Look back over pages 87 to 89 and pick out three other ways in which Sugden is cruel to Billy. Remember them in the next section, where Sugden traps Billy in the shower.

After putting on the shorts, Billy runs out to the field to play football. First, Sugden organizes picking the teams. He and Tibbut are captains, and of course Sugden picks all the best players. Billy isn't one of these and is left until the end. Read that section through, and think back to a time when perhaps you have suffered through not being chosen for something. How do you think Billy feels?

The remaining preparations for the game are as follows. Sugden takes off his tracksuit and is mocked by the boys. Then Sugden challenges Billy about the position he is playing in, and puts him in goal. Why do you think Billy is so unwilling to be goalkeeper? Finally, under pressure, Tibbut decides that his team is Spurs (what is so funny about this?). Then the game begins.

As you read the account of the game, from pages 94 to 103, have four questions in your mind. First, ask yourself what it shows us about Sugden, particularly about his being a frustrated footballer. See what you can learn about Billy. Thirdly, think of how the game seemed to one of the other players – Tibbut, for example. Lastly, see how the match compares with any games that you might have played during P.E. lessons at school.

Once you have read the account, see if you can remember the order in which things happen during the match. Can you put these in the right sequence?

1. Billy calmed the dog and led it off the field.
2. Sugden let the ball go over the line, to the boys' disgust.
3. Billy climbed the netting and pretended he was an animal.
4. Billy let the ball in for the first time.
5. Billy wanted to go for lunch and Sugden refused.
6. Billy jumped from the bar.
7. Sugden hit Billy with the ball.

8. Billy let a second goal in.
9. A dog ran on to the field.
10. Sugden scored a penalty.
11. Sugden allowed an offside goal.
12. Sugden stopped Tibbut shooting by tugging his shirt.
13. Billy let the final goal in.
14. The winning goal suddenly became important.
15. Billy saved a goal.

When you have put what happened during the match in the right order, go back and ask yourself the questions we mentioned before. First, what part does Sugden play in the match? We know from descriptions of his play that he is not that good at football – and that his age doesn't help. How many references to this can you find? Sugden also cheats, and uses his position as teacher to draw all the attention to himself as referee, commentator and star player. Sugden also picks on Billy. Look at the times they speak to each other. In almost every case, Sugden is on the attack and so Billy answers him back. Even when Billy helps out by leading the dog off the pitch, Sugden is not happy. Make notes on Sugden and the impresson he makes on you.

What did the other boys think of the game, particularly if they were in Tibbut's side? Where boys in Sugden and Billy's side must have been annoyed with Billy for letting that last goal in, those on Tibbut's side might have been pleased. Using the list of incidents in the match, invent a conversation between Tibbut and a boy from another class in which Tibbut describes the match. How do you think he felt when Sugden cheated? Notice how his feelings changed when 'the winning goal suddenly became important' (p. 101). What did Tibbut think when Billy let the final goal in?

SECTION 17, pp. 103–8

When the game is over, Billy rushes off to the changing room and puts his clothes on. Sugden, though, is after revenge. He tackles Billy, pointing out that the boy hasn't had a shower. Billy says, 'I've had one, Sir.'

Sugden hits him, calls him a liar (has Billy lied?), and then checks with the others. When no one can prove that Billy has showered and Billy can't produce a note from his mother, Sugden orders him to undress and shower.

When Billy is undressed, he is obviously filthy. Read the description of him on page 105, and see if you can form a clear idea of him in your mind. Barry Hines says he is like 'a child hurrying towards the final solution'. In other words, he looks like a child in a concentration camp.

Once Billy is in the shower, Sugden blocks him at one end and tells three other boys to block him at the other. Then he turns the water to cold, and keeps Billy in the freezing shower.

During this whole incident, lots of things happen that can be seen to be wrong.

Who does the following:

1. Lies by saying he has had a shower.
2. Hits Billy across the cheek.
3. Argues with Mr Sugden.
4. Lies by saying he has a cold.
5. Bullies Billy with words.
6. Makes Billy have a shower.
7. Blocks one end of the shower on Sugden's orders.
8. Hits Billy with wet towels.
9. Turns the shower to cold.
10. Denies having seen Billy have a shower.

Go down the list again. Pick out those actions that you think are wrong. Then write down why you think each action is wrong. Are any excusable? Do you think the people who performed them think they are wrong?

Write down a few sentences to continue each of these defences:

I don't think I was wrong to lie about having a shower because ...

I don't think I was wrong to turn on the cold shower tap because ...

I don't think I was wrong to block the shower when Sugden told me to because ...

At last, even though the water is freezing, Billy stops yelling. It is this that shuts the other boys up. What do you think they are thinking? Do they argue with Sugden?

Just as everyone is beginning to be worried – notice how they've become more sympathetic to Billy during the day – Billy appears over the shower partition. Everyone laughs with relief. Sugden lets him go. Billy dresses quickly and rushes home.

Look at how Billy handles the incident of the cold shower. He puts up with it, and, because he does, the boys cheer him. His final leap over the partition is a victory. He escapes, Sugden has to let him go, and Billy wins.

SECTION 18, pp. 108–21

Billy rushes straight home, greets Kes and then goes to get her food. He has a board, a knife and some meat in the garage, but he also decides to kill a sparrow to give Kes fresh meat.

Billy gets Jud's air rifle. As he is doing this, he notices Jud's betting slip and money on the mantelpiece. He doesn't want to take the bet to the shop and decides whether or not to do so by flipping a coin. There is a good description of Billy loading, aiming and firing the rifle on pages 109 to 110. Read it through and get a clear idea of what he is doing.

The coin comes down tails – so Billy reluctantly puts the slip and money into his pocket. But before going to the betting shop he sees to Kes. (What does this show us about Billy's priorities?)

Billy has obviously shot sparrows before, for he has a spot set up in the garage to sight them. He sees one, but it flies off. Then he sights another.

Read the passages where Billy shoots the sparrow. It starts with a description of the live sparrow, the way it looks and moves. When Billy sights the sparrow, it hears him and looks around. Billy freezes until the bird feels safe. Finally, Billy adjusts the rifle and fires. The sparrow falls and Billy goes out to pick up the body. He is interested in the lack of marks where the bullet has entered and fires a slug into the ground to see if that leaves a mark.

There is a real contradiction in this passage. Billy loves Kes – and we know from earlier in the book and from his later conversation with Mr Farthing that he loves other animals too. Yet he still kills the sparrow. Why do you think he does? How can he calmly kill it, yet later be so upset over Kes?

Taking everything he needs – use the glossary and check that you know what all the things are that Billy takes with him – he goes to Kes. He eases her onto the glove, secures her and then takes her out, just as he described to the class.

Once in the field, Billy lets Kes go and swings the lure. Kes is just about to fly for the lure when a shout interrupts them. It is Mr Farthing. Letting Kes take the lure, Billy turns to him, at first annoyed, then stubbornly patient. In this situation things are the other way round, and Mr Farthing obeys Billy's orders. Why?

With Farthing watching, Billy flies Kes to the lure. It is a wonderful description (p. 113). Read it through more than once, and imagine it clearly – each sound, each movement.

Can you see Billy letting the hawk go for the lure, then whisking it out of reach at the last moment? Can you hear him calling her back? Maybe you can feel how Mr Farthing felt as he watched, and how Billy felt as he flew Kes.

Imagine you are Mr Farthing. Write an account of what you saw, as if you were describing it to a friend later that night. Don't copy the words Barry Hines uses to describe Kes flying. Use your own, just as if you were talking to someone you know.

When Kes has taken the lure (p. 114), Billy turns to Mr Farthing. He immediately shows how much he enjoyed the experience – 'Brilliant!' – and then nearly gets his fingers raked by the hawk's claws.

Billy gives Kes the dead sparrow to eat. The description of how Kes eats it is not very pleasant, but it is accurate and certainly makes an impression. Why do you think Barry Hines includes it in the book? Read these reasons – do you think any of them are close to the truth?

1. Barry Hines wants to make his readers feel sick.
2. He wants to shock his readers to make them react strongly to the book.
3. He means to show us that the hawk is a cruel bird.
4. He is demonstrating that the law of nature is about one species living off another.
5. He is including violence because it is popular nowadays.

6. He wants to show us something about Billy and his reaction to Kes.
7. He wants to show us something of Mr Farthing's character.

Can you find anything you like about the description? Do your best to find one thing.

Pages 116 to 119 are about Mr Farthing's talk with Billy about the hawk. This is similar in some ways to the talk they had after the fight (pp. 80–85), but there are also differences. Think of as many as you can, taking these phrases as clues:

1. The situation: where they are.
2. Who is in charge.
3. How Mr Farthing treats Billy.
4. How Billy treats Mr Farthing.
5. What they talk about.

You can learn a lot about Billy and Mr Farthing from this conversation. Add it to what you already know. Also, compare Billy's conversation with Mr Farthing to any time you might have met a teacher out of school time. Were you able to talk to them more easily or not?

The main topic of conversation is Kes, and hawks. What is said here tells us a lot about falconry and how it affects people. Read through the section again, pages 116 to 119, and jot down any words which tell you about Billy's love of hawks and of Kes in particular. Why does he love the bird? What does he feel when he flies Kes?

At last Mr Farthing has to go back to school. He offers Billy a lift which he refuses, but even so they seem to get on well. Perhaps for the first time ever, Billy feels an adult has time for him. Mr Farthing has seen the real, confident, skilful Billy and not the useless class clown everyone else seems to see.

What might have happened if Farthing had carried on encouraging Billy? If the class had built on the sympathy they had started to have for him? If Billy had got better at being proud of himself and talking to adults as equals? Write a few lines saying what might have happened if the book had developed happily.

The last part of this section sees Billy crumbling a pellet. The pellet is a result of Kes's eating another sparrow perhaps, a while ago.

We are seeing what happens when one animal has eaten another –

and it is almost as horrible as the description of Kes eating the sparrow. Then we see Billy hurting himself by pinching a bone between finger and thumb. Why does Barry Hines include this? Does it perhaps show Billy bringing himself back down to earth after the intense excitement of flying Kes and gaining Mr Farthing's warm approval?

SECTION 19, pp. 121–6

This section opens with a description of the part of the estate round the betting shop. It shows us how very ugly it is – nature does burst through on this patch of waste ground, as we see from the mention of grass and bushes, but it is soon destroyed by litter and neglect.

Billy is on his way to place Jud's bet. He wondered earlier whether to or not, but something decided him to do as Jud wanted – can you remember what? But now, smelling the fish and chips, he wonders again, tosses a coin, loses, tosses again and takes the best of three. Have you ever tossed a coin to decide anything? How did it feel? Heads he loses and so he should take the bet. He swears and carries on to the shop. He nearly gets knocked down by a man rushing out of the betting shop, then opens the door and goes in.

The inside of the shop is described carefully to give us a good sense of atmosphere. The shop is almost empty, but everyone there is absorbed in placing their bets. It is another example of Barry Hines's very accurate observation.

Billy approaches one of the men, who is writing a betting slip. He wants to know whether the two horses Jud has chosen have a chance of winning; if not, he can safely spend the money himself, and Jud will never know. The man tells him that one horse probably will win, but the other has no chance. Billy makes up his mind. He throws the slip into the fire and leaves the shop.

The second half of this section tells us what Billy does with Jud's money. First he goes into the fish and chip shop. Is this shop like chip shops you have seen? What differences are there?

The lady in the chip shop is kind to Billy, giving him extra chips and some scraps. Life is getting better for him. Compare this with Mr Porter's treatment of him.

In the butcher's, the same thing happens. It is as if, having talked to Mr Farthing and started being friendly with people for the first time, Billy is able to be human. He gives the butcher a chip and the butcher gives him some meat for free. Billy then buys some cigarettes – no need to steal, now he has money – and goes back to school.

This section is rather sad, despite the fact that things seem to be improving for Billy; the axe is about to fall.

Why does disaster strike at this point? What causes the events that follow? As you read on, remember that everything stems from Billy's failure to place Jud's bet. Whose fault is this – Jud's, Billy's, anyone else's? Is it just chance?

SECTION 20, pp. 126–35

It is afternoon, and becoming stormy. The lights are on in the school rooms and everyone is at work. Barry Hines mentions some typical scenes – classrooms, offices, the foyer. Do they remind you of any familiar scenes at school?

Billy's class is doing maths. The room is quiet and Billy begins to fall asleep. He is woken by the teacher calling his name, but drifts off again into another daydream.

What happens now is the beginning of a series of events that are broken only by the interview with the Employment Officer and finally ended by Billy's discovery of Kes's death. Jud is out to take his revenge.

In the middle of his daydream, Billy thinks he sees Jud coming up the school drive. At first he is not sure and rubs the window pane to get a clearer view, but sees nothing.

From this moment on, Billy is terrified. Notice how he shows this. Barry Hines builds up the suspense, only allowing us to breathe again when Jud has left the school and Billy returns to his class (p. 133).

Read the next few pages and notice first of all how we are kept aware of Billy's growing fear. Find the occasions when Billy does the following things, all showing us that he is terrified. Then arrange them in the order in which they happen in the book.

1. Hides in the boiler room.

2. Runs from Jud into the toilets.
3. Starts to cry.
4. Hides under coats in the cloakroom.
5. Races under the school's windows.
6. Checks with other boys to find out if they've seen Jud.
7. Flattens himself against a wall.
8. Goes very pale as the boys watch him.
9. Waits to leave the classroom with the teacher.

You now know how Billy reacted to Jud. Write about this from Billy's point of view. Begin: 'As soon as I saw Jud coming up the school path...' Include as many words as you can to describe how Billy felt as well as what he was doing. You may like to remind yourself of any times you've been afraid, and how that felt.

Describing Billy's fear is one way Barry Hines uses to build up suspense in this section. There are other ways – how many can you spot? Be particularly aware of how he uses sound (like the noise of Jud's footsteps approaching the classroom door) and how he uses near-miss situations (like Billy's escaping from Jud by walking with the teacher).

During the chase, we don't take Jud's point of view at all. How do you think he feels when he is walking up the school path – and as he chases Billy round the school? What does this show us of Billy and Jud's relationship?

Eventually Billy has to run for it through the school, finally finding refuge in the boiler room.

When Billy wakes up after his doze in the boiler room, he at first finds the door locked, but quickly springs the lock (what does this tell us about Billy?) and goes back into school to find his class. He stares into one classroom for so long that the teacher comes out. Billy lies effortlessly to explain what he is doing. Then the bell goes, and Billy is able to track his class down and mingle with them. How are we able to tell that he is relieved?

Billy is in for a shock, though. Tibbut answers his questions about Jud, and then tells him that he should have been at the Youth Employment interview (where did we hear about this before?).

When Gryce meets him at the door of the classroom, he is obviously angry. He shows his character clearly in the way he speaks to Billy, hits him, shows no sympathy for him. What do you learn about Gryce from this? – add these notes to those you have already made about the headmaster. Notice, too, how easily Billy lies to protect himself, and keeps out of reach of the headmaster.

In the end, Billy actually wins. In trying to hit him, Gryce loses his balance and his dignity. The boys don't dare to laugh, so avoid each other's eyes. To let off steam, Gryce viciously cuffs a small boy as he passes. What is the difference between someone like Gryce and a bully like MacDowall? What is the difference between Gryce's hitting Billy on this occasion, and Farthing's hitting MacDowall after the fight?

Notice how impossible it is for Billy to ask for help in school. He cannot get help from the maths teacher, and Tibbut betrays him by pointing him out to Jud. When he is missing from class, no one is worried – and Gryce sums everything up by his meeting with Billy at the end of the section. School, for Billy, is a disaster.

SECTION 21, pp. 135–40

The first part of this section, Billy's interview with the Youth Employment Officer, is the final one in the setting of the school. It also gives us an idea of what Billy's future is going to be like after he leaves school. The second part shows us, after Billy slowly realizes what Jud might have done, his discovery that Kes has gone. This is the point at which Billy's future turns black. We are reminded that, if Kes has gone, Billy has nothing left but a life down the pit.

Billy waits outside the medical room for his interview. He overhears another boy and his mother, about to go in for the interview, arguing with each other. As they go into the medical room, another boy and his mother come out and walk off talking. How do you think Billy feels about this? Is he triumphant that his mother isn't there to nag him? How else might he feel?

When he is alone, Billy has nothing to do but look around him – at the tiled floor, at his feet on the floor, at the skid marks, at the fire alarm – which he taps and rubs. At first there seems no point in these descriptive paragraphs, but they do show us something about Billy: can you think what? They also add to the school atmosphere.

When the woman and the boy come out of the interview room,

the Employment Officer calls Billy in. Read the interview, which is described on pages 137 to 140.

What should an interview for career advice be like? It is aimed at helping young people find out what their strengths are and guiding them into the right sort of job. But it is obvious that this interview does nothing of the sort for Billy. On the surface, the Employment Officer does all the right things – suggests jobs, asks about hobbies, gives Billy a leaflet. Write down the things the Youth Employment Officer says and does that have the opposite effect to the one he is trying to create – that make Billy resentful, show a lack of understanding of his skills and ignore what he can do.

Read the Employment Officer's long speech on pages 138 to 139. Do you think Billy listens to this? Is it of any use to him?

Think of any careers advice interviews you may have been to. Were they like this one? Were they different? Write down five things that would make a careers advice interview of real use. Then rewrite the account of Billy's interview with the Youth Employment Officer so that the interview is a useful one. What might the officer discover about Billy that would convince him that Billy had potential? What job might Billy be guided to by the end of it?

Next, think about what sort of person you think the Youth Employment Officer is. Barry Hines includes a very clear physical description of him, stressing his baldness, to show how very different he is from Billy. Write down five other ways in which the Youth Employment Officer differs from Billy – and therefore cannot understand him.

Then look at how Billy handles the situation. He realizes immediately that the interview is not going to help him, but plays along with it until the man suggests going down the pit. How does he react then? And what does this show about him?

It is the question about hobbies that finally makes Billy realize that Kes may be in danger. This is not stated directly in the book. We simply notice that when Billy hears the question he immediately asks to leave the interview. It takes a moment before we realize why. Even then, the Youth Employment Officer's filling in the form and handing Billy a leaflet distract us from Billy's real thoughts. What are his real thoughts?

When he leaves the medical room, Billy just rushes out of school and runs home. Why do you think Barry Hines does not describe the run in detail, but just brings us, in one sentence, to Billy's home?

Notice how he brings us directly to the words, 'The hawk was gone.'

From this point on, through the end of this section to the middle of the next, Billy's one thought is to find Kes. His first action is to shout the hawk's name.

Then he rushes round the house, up to the bedroom and down again, calling Jud. But Jud isn't there, so Billy has to go out with the lure to call Kes. First he works the field, then, when he is tired, runs back and out across the road in front of his house, meeting a woman whom he asks about Jud. What do you think Billy is thinking and feeling at that moment? Barry Hines does not tell us — he lets us imagine, and that is far more effective than doing it for us. Write down five things you imagine Billy is feeling as he searches the house and calls Jud.

Compare this with the time, earlier that day, when he happily worked Kes to the lure for Mr Farthing. What are the differences — and how does the contrast between the two occasions make you feel?

SECTION 22, pp. 142–50

Billy now learns what has really happened by going to the bookmaker's shop. Which of the following accounts is nearest to what Mrs Rose, the bookmaker's wife, tells Billy?

1. That Jud had realized Billy hadn't put the bet on and had gone to the bookmaker's shop to check on this.
2. That Jud had not realized that Billy hadn't put the bet on and had gone to the bookmaker's shop to collect his money.
3. That Jud had gone to the bookmaker's shop to collect his money, had not believed them when they said Billy hadn't put the bet on, but had finally been convinced.
4. Jud had gone to the bookmaker's shop to collect his money and had got angry when they wouldn't pay him the odds he said the horses were worth.

Billy is obviously shattered by the news Mrs Rose has for him. He starts to cry, and the woman warns him of Jud's anger and his threat of revenge. Billy still hopes that Jud has simply let the bird go. He runs off into the fields to work the lure again. Over the next few pages, up to page 146, he searches for Kes – not simply in one field, as he did earlier, but over a stile, through the woods, and over to Monastery Farm. At one point he loses the lure, but gets it back on his return to the estate.

This section is a mixture of detailed description – the rain, the trees, the grass, the skies – and of Billy's emotions. These are shown by his frantic whirling of the lure, his calling 'Kes! Kes!' over and over again, his desperate running and blundering across fields and through woods. Read the section again, noticing how Barry Hines shows us what Billy is feeling while at the same time showing us how important nature is to him.

Have you ever lost something or someone that is very important to you? Have you ever searched for it, or tried to get it back? How did you feel? What did you do? Remembering how Barry Hines showed us Billy's desperation, write a paragraph describing your situation and how you reacted.

Having reached Monastery Farm, Billy stares at it for a while. What do you think he remembers, and what might he be hoping for by going back there? He is disappointed. Kes is not there, so he slowly makes his way back through the woods. He starts to see the lights of the estate, and reaches his house.

Before he goes in, though, with a last hope he takes a look into the shed. It is empty. He goes back to the house.

You can imagine how Billy is feeling as he bursts into the house. He stands up to Jud as he never has before. He is desperate, breathing heavily, and furiously angry.

In contrast, their mother behaves very differently. Barry Hines makes this contrast even clearer by describing the room with all its normal everyday detail, which is so very different from the once-in-a-lifetime trauma Billy is going through.

What do you think their mother is thinking and feeling? Divide these descriptions into two lists, one for each person. Then use the lists to write about how Jud and Billy's mum behaves during this section of the book.

1. Violent towards Billy – threatens him with a poker.
2. Nervous but defensive.
3. Vaguely concerned about Billy's health.

4. Embarrassed at Billy's emotion.
5. Prepared to hit Billy for using bad language.
6. Furiously angry at Billy for what the boy has done.
7. Irritable with Billy for staring.
8. Shocked that Jud has killed the hawk.
9. Cross with Billy for not placing the bet.
10. Regretful for what has been lost.

After you have thought about how Jud and Billy's mum have behaved, you might like to consider how wrong they are. Can you think of any reasons for their behaving in this way? After you have done this, write a paragraph as if Jud was speaking, beginning: 'Well, of course, I was angry...', and a paragraph as if Billy's mum was speaking, starting with the words: 'Well, I didn't know what had happened...' Give what you think Jud's and Billy's mum's reasons might be for their actions.

During all this, Billy goes from anger – shouting at Jud to make him say where Kes is – to tears. He tries to go to his mum for comfort, but she will not have anything to do with him and tells him not to be 'so daft' (p. 149). This is a very important moment – it is the only time in the book that Billy turns to anyone else for help – and he is rejected.

Then Jud finally admits he has killed Kes because the bird attacked him, and Billy can stand no more. He rushes at Jud, swears at him, and then appeals to his mother for support – which is not forthcoming.

Eventually Jud admits that he has put Kes in the dustbin. Billy rushes out. It is a very sad scene indeed when he takes Kes's body from the bin and looks at it, blowing the feathers and touching them lightly.

Can you imagine what Billy is feeling at this time? He has lost more than a pet; what has he lost? Write down five things that Billy has lost, now that he no longer has Kes. Then write about what you think Billy is thinking and feeling as he stands holding Kes's body.

SECTION 23, pp. 150–53

Billy carries Kes's body back into the house. You might think that, faced with what he has done, Jud might be sorry, or that their mother would support Billy. But in the end, neither of them understands or realizes what the bird means to him.

Jud has already done his worst. Billy turns to his mother, hoping to get her sympathy and support. He shows her the bird – and at first she seems to back him up. Find three sentences spoken by Billy's mum that show she at least tries to sympathize. She even tries to tell Jud off. But in the end she can't do anything. Billy wants his mum to punish Jud for what has happened, but she isn't powerful enough. Jud calls her bluff.

Billy's mum has had enough and turns on Billy for crying. In the final betrayal, she says, '. . . it's only a bird. You can get another can't you?'

If you were Billy, what would be your reaction at this point? Is it only a bird? Can he get another? Write down what your own reactions to her comments would have been if you had been Billy.

What he does in fact is to hit out at his mother – the first time he has done so. He then follows this with an attack on both Jud and their mother, furniture and crockery flying. When they both go for him, Billy swings Kes at them – his final gesture – and heads for the door.

Billy's mother calls him and then comes up the path after him, but he runs on. The neighbours cluster round to watch him as he goes.

Why do you think Barry Hines includes this scene in the book? Isn't it enough that Jud kills the hawk? Why is it almost worse that Billy's mother does not understand how important Kes is to him?

How does her betrayal affect Billy? Up to this point we thought things were going better for him, as he talked to Mr Farthing and got free meat from the butcher. Now he reacts violently; how do you feel he will react to people from now on?

Imagine Billy's mother was a different kind of person. What could she have done that would have helped Billy, even if she could not bring Kes back? What could she have said or done that might have prevented him from becoming so completely violent and disillusioned? What would you say to Billy if you met him as he was running away from the house, carrying Kes?

SECTION 24, pp. 153–60

Once away from the house, Billy slows down. He puts Kes's body in
the pocket of his big jacket. Then he walks round the estate, round and
round. The estate is described in detail, all the houses the same, nothing
really cared for, everything ugly. What is Barry Hines saying in giving
us this detailed description? What does he want us to feel about the
estate, the surroundings that Billy lives in and their effect on Billy?

There are very few people around – and no one is interested in Billy.
He passes his schoolmates' houses, but he cannot go to them for help.
He goes past Porter's shop and it is closed. There is no one Billy can
turn to. Who is the only person who might be able to help him? Why
do you think he doesn't go to this person for help?

Finally, Billy reaches an old cinema, the Palace. This place has not
been mentioned before in the book – we don't know yet why it is
important. But Billy starts to remember, and makes up his mind to
break in. The description of the cinema and of how Billy does manage
to break in may well remind you of old cinemas you have seen – or even
of a time when you found your way into an old, empty building. If so,
how does your experience compare with Billy's? Is it the same? What
are the differences in what you saw and heard? How did you feel?

If you have never been inside an old, deserted building, you might
like to imagine how Billy feels. Barry Hines doesn't tell us directly, but
the fact that Billy explores the place and stays for a while probably
means that he is not too scared.

Once Billy has explored the cinema, he finds a seat cushion and sits
down. In the darkness, with only the hum of the distant traffic, he
begins to remember being in the cinema when he was a little boy.

This final part of Kes, when Billy is remembering what happened
when he was small, is one of the most important parts of the book. It
tells us a lot about why Billy is as he is.

He remembers being at the cinema with his dad, and all the nice
things he saw, heard, smelled and tasted. Everything was somehow
brighter and better then, when he was with his dad.

Then he remembers walking home, his dad suddenly seeing a
friend's car outside the house and realizing – though little Billy didn't
understand – that his mum was having an affair. Billy's dad hit 'Uncle
Mick', and then there was a lot of screaming and shouting; later, while

Billy was in bed, his dad packed his suitcase and left. He deserted his family.

Moments in the cinema are possibly the last bits of happiness Billy can remember in his life up to the time he had Kes. It also shows us what life could have been like had his dad still been there – we are sure that Billy feels that life would have been happy. We also suspect that the upset of seeing the scene between his dad and 'Uncle Mick', and of his dad leaving, has affected Billy, though in what ways we can never be sure. Certainly if he had had someone to love him – as he remembers his dad doing and as he has loved Kes, but as his mum and Jud can never do – life would have been different.

Now Billy's fantasy turns to revenge. If only he were the hero of the Big Picture, and Kes were alive again. He imagines Jud as the quarry and Kes, the bird of prey, stooping on him. But it doesn't happen like that. Kes misses, Jud runs. The picture continues, and once more Kes stoops – but again she misses. Kes is dead, and Jud has won.

Unable even in his imagination to make things all right, Billy has nothing left. He runs out of the cinema and, with a last shudder, walks away. When he gets home to an empty house he buries Kes and goes to bed.

This ending seems a very unhappy one. Billy cannot even imagine winning – he is totally beaten. Finally, he accepts that Kes has gone, and simply goes to bed. We imagine him waking up next morning, just as he woke at the start of the book, to a cold dawn. What do you think Barry Hines is trying to tell us with such an ending? How do you think he is trying to make us feel – and why?

Just as, at the start of the book, we looked at the way in which the author introduced us to the story, so at the end we need to look at how Barry Hines rounds off the book.

Like the conclusions of most pieces of writing, the final section of *Kes* sets out to do many things. When you have read it, pick out from the following list the things it does. Do you think it does them successfully?

1. Completes the story for us.
2. Helps us to a better understanding of Billy's reactions.
3. Gives us a happy ending.
4. Brings the story full circle.

5. Ends the day the story began with.
6. Leaves us with a feeling of completion.
7. Brings many of the ideas of the story together and links them.
8. Hints at what Billy's future will be.
9. Gives us a final clue that helps the various parts of the story to fall into place.
10. Surprises us with the ending.

As you look back over the book, having worked through it, you might also like to consider whether you liked it or not. Which were the least successful parts for you, and which the most successful? Which characters did you like and which did you hate? Did you find anything in it that helped you understand your own situation better?

Characters

BILLY CASPER

Billy, of course, is the hero of the novel. He is the centre of the book and appears in every scene. Everything goes on around him. As we read the novel, we get very involved with Billy and what he does. At the end of the book, when Kes is killed and Billy's world falls apart, we really feel sorry for him.

The first thing we find out about Billy is the situation he lives in. He has been brought up in a mining village in a poor family which is not happy. And through the book we discover other things about Billy's life. Here is a list of five of them. List them in the order in which they happened, and then use them to write about Billy's life up to the start of *Kes*.

1. Billy's dad left home.
2. Billy, his mum, dad and Jud lived happily.
3. Billy's dad discovered that his mum was having an affair.
4. Billy got more disruptive and was in trouble with the police.
5. Billy started to train Kes.

During the book, we see that Billy does not have a happy life. Look at his life at home: his brother bullies him, and his mum doesn't care for him. What are the worst things that you notice when you read about Billy's life at home? How do you think they affect him?

What is Billy's relationship with Jud like? Jud almost always treats Billy violently. Billy veers between trying to keep on the good side of Jud, and trying to fight back. How do you think Billy feels about Jud? If you were to ask Billy about Jud, what would he probably say?

Billy does not get any support from his mum, and he certainly plays her up and answers her back. But he still needs her. Look particularly at the final sections of the book, where Billy faces Jud and his mum with Kes's dead body. Find clues to Billy's feelings about his mum – his need for her still, and for her help. Then think about the way Billy's mum reacts to all these. Do you think this affects Billy? Does it change him?

Outside home, Billy is not much happier. His school doesn't do much for him either. He can hardly read and write, is no good at sports, and is seen as a scoundrel and a clown by almost all the teachers and the Youth Employment Officer. Only one teacher seems to have any time for him and that is Mr Farthing, when he finds out about Kes. Even his schoolmates think Billy is odd and laugh at him, though through the events of the day on which *Kes* is set they begin to see another side of him.

Imagine you are writing Billy's school profile when he leaves. Put in comments by Crossley his form master, Farthing his English teacher, Sugden the games master, and the Youth Employment Officer. Put in a comment by the headmaster, Gryce. Finally, imagine you are one of the boys in his class, and add your comments. How would you sum up the impression Billy gives at school?

He is none too successful outside school. He still steals occasionally. Mr Porter doesn't trust him, and the neighbours think that he and his family are violent and strange. And although, just before Kes's death, things seem to be looking up, in the end no one helps Billy.

All this tells us how Billy is with other people. He seems dull, dishonest, silly and occasionally violent. Certainly he lies and steals easily. How many examples of Billy's lying, cheating, stealing and violence can you find in the book? How many things can you find Billy doing that he is punished for?

Now read through what you have written and decide which of the things Billy did are, in your opinion, really wrong. He certainly thinks he is picked on, and that he can never keep out of trouble even when he behaves; is he right?

The only happy things in Billy's life seem to be nature and Kes. He has cared for many animals in the past, but Kes is special. He really loves the bird and this shows in lots of ways. He puts her first, rushing home at lunchtime to feed her and taking great care in her training. His feelings also show when he is talking about her. Look at the three times he does this and pick out clues that show Billy's feelings about Kes.

Now make two lists, one of things which Billy does for, or gives, Kes, the other of things having Kes does for Billy. How many can you think of?

You should certainly have mentioned the fact that having Kes gives Billy a sense of pride and power. This shows clearly when he takes her out. Also, it is obvious that Billy is an expert with the bird, as Mr Farthing says. When he is with Kes he does well. He is skilled. He is proud of himself – which he isn't anywhere else in his life.

When Kes is killed Billy loses all this, and he loses the only thing in his life that he loves. What effect does this have on him? Pair off the following phrases so that they show how Billy was while Kes was alive, and how he seems once she is dead:

    has something to love
    has some hope
    has a skill
    is only slightly violent
    has something to work for

    has no motivation in life
    does not control his violence
    has no hope
    has nothing to show his skill
    has nothing to love

We learn a little more about Billy when, after Kes's death, he goes to the old cinema and remembers his dad. This helps us to understand what the turning point in Billy's childhood was. Now he has lost the only other thing he loved – and, as we see from the final pages, this is too much for him.

There are some last questions to ask about Billy. The first is to ask yourself whether you like him or not. If you met him while he had Kes, how would you feel about him? Could you talk to him? What would you say? What if you met him after he had lost Kes?

Finally, what do you think the future is going to be like for Billy? Is there any way it could be brighter? What job will he do when he leaves school? Will he end up like Jud? Will he go back to stealing again? Will he ever get another hawk? We don't know – but you can think of your own answers to these questions, and work out Billy's future for yourself.

JUD

Jud, Billy's brother, is the villain of the piece. It is hard to find anything good to say about him, and maybe we are meant to see him like this – as just a villain.

Jud appears in the book more than anyone else except Kes and Billy, and every time we see him he is causing trouble. We see him going to work, then taking revenge on Billy by chasing him round the school, and then killing Kes. Also Billy remembers Jud's mockery and drunkenness on the day Billy first took Kes.

Jud himself works at the pit. Can you imagine what sort of life this is? How does Jud feel about it? He mentions it several times, and we see, when he comes home late one evening, what he does with his spare time. His cannot be much of a life.

All this results in a Jud who is a nasty person. We only see him with his mum and Billy – and he ill-treats both of them. Read through the descriptions of Jud on pages 37 to 39 and page 147, and make notes on how he behaves to his mum. It is obvious that he has the upper hand and she is almost afraid of him. How do we know this? Imagining you are Billy's mum, write a paragraph saying what you think and feel about Jud.

To Billy, Jud is a monster. Make a list of all the ways in which Jud bullies Billy, from little things, like taking the bedclothes off, to the worst of all – killing Kes. Why do you think Jud does these things? Does he have a reason? Have you ever known anyone like Jud – and if so, how did you feel about that person?

Jud's final action, killing Kes, is really brutal. And he does not really seem to care, even when it is obvious that Billy is shattered by what he has done. Is there anything you could say (or do) to Jud which might help him realize what he has done, and stop him behaving like this again?

Jud is the villain of the book, but there may be some things which could make us sorry for him. We are not told clearly what sort of childhood he had, but if you read through the book looking for clues you might be able to work out for yourself what Jud's past must have been like. Write down a short account of what Jud's life might have been like up to the time the book starts, and then see if anything you have written makes you feel sorry for him.

Jud has to be in the book. For several reasons, it could not be the same without him. Rearrange these reasons, putting the one you consider most important first, and so on. There are two red herrings which aren't true – miss them out.

1. Jud shows us what Billy might grow up to be.
2. Billy and Jud argue – this adds to the excitement of the book.
3. The way Jud changes in the course of the book is interesting.
4. Jud shows us what Billy is like by the way the boy reacts to him.
5. Jud chasing Billy round the school adds to the surprises of the book.
6. Jud's relationship with his mum tells us something about Billy's family.
7. Jud gives us someone in the book to hate.
8. Jud's killing Kes is the climax of the book.
9. Jud's killing Kes makes us feel deep emotion.
10. Jud's descriptions of life down the pit are an important part of the book.

Now use these reasons to write a paragraph beginning, 'Jud is important in *Kes* because...'. Add any other reasons of your own you can think of.

Final questions to ask about Jud are: What will happen to him after the book ends? Will he carry on working at the pit? Will he leave home? Will his life change in any way?

BILLY'S MUM

We learn something about Billy's mum on four occasions in the book – pages 18 to 21, 37 to 38, 147 to 152 and 158 to 159. Look through these sections again carefully before you read on.

The first time we meet Billy's mum is on the morning of the day the book covers. She is going off to work, and she and Billy fight because he refuses to go to the shop to buy cigarettes for her. We then remember her, as Billy does, mocking him for wanting to have a kestrel when he first got Kes. When Jud eventually kills the bird, Billy's mum cannot respond to Billy at all, cannot help him, and does not really understand why he is upset. We learn at the end of the book that Billy's father left in the first place because of his wife's affairs with other men – something which is still continuing.

So we know that Billy's mum was once married and living with her husband, Jud and Billy, but that because she had a boyfriend her husband left her. You might like to begin by imagining how Billy's dad felt about this – and then by wondering how Billy's mum felt when her husband left her.

From this point on, she had to cope on her own. Make a list of the difficulties Billy's mum might have had to deal with when she was bringing up her two sons. Think of practical difficulties – for example, she doesn't seem to have any real friends. Now write a paragraph as if you were Billy's mum, explaining why it was not really your fault that Jud has turned out violent and that Billy has been in trouble for stealing. Try to be as sympathetic as you can towards her.

But on the whole, Billy's mum is not a very likeable person. When you have read through all the sections that mention her, make a list of all the things you don't like about her. Give examples of things she does that make you dislike her. Have you ever known anyone like her – and how did you feel about that person?

Think about how far Billy's mum is responsible for Kes's being killed. What did she do – to Billy, to Jud – that made it happen? What did she not do that she could have done? There are several ways in which she could have helped Billy after Kes was killed. So how far is Billy's mum responsible for what happens to Billy at the very end of the book?

Billy's mum is actually a very interesting character to have in a book. As well as making things happen, she stirs up strong emotions in us and makes us sympathize with Billy even more strongly. She helps us to realize that Billy's problems are caused by the people around him as much as by himself – and that family life, which could be so supportive, can actually be destructive. Remember that Billy's mum has brought Jud and Billy up, and taught them many of the things they now know and do.

FARTHING

Mr Farthing is an unusual person. He is the only one in the book who seems to be on Billy's side, and to want to help in any real way.

We first meet him on page 58, taking Billy's class for English. It is obvious that he is a better teacher than, for example, Sugden. Look at the way he controls the boys, yet manages to get them interested in the lesson. He is really the one teacher who makes us feel that school has any point for Billy. Imagine you are one of the boys in Farthing's English class, and write down what you think of him as a teacher. Include your criticisms as well as what you feel are the good things about him.

Farthing is particularly effective when he encourages Billy to talk about Kes. Notice how here – and later, after the fight and at Billy's house – he really listens to him and shows his interest. Farthing treats Billy as an equal when Billy is talking about something only he knows about.

What effect does Farthing have on Billy? Read particularly the sections where they talk alone; make a list of ten things Billy says or does that he doesn't do when he is with other people. Are all these good things – does Farthing affect Billy in a good way?

There is only one part of the book where Farthing seems to be less of a good man, and that is when he attacks MacDowall after the fight in the playground. Think again about why he might have done this, and whether you blame him. Everyone in the book seems to use violence as a way of coping. Do you think Farthing does too?

But all in all, Farthing seems to be one of the nicest people in the book. Why do you think Barry Hines includes one helpful person?

By the time Farthing leaves Billy at lunchtime, we really feel he has helped him and that there is hope for Billy. What do you think Farthing feels? Perhaps he is very hopeful for Billy too.

Of course, things go wrong. It is certainly true that Billy's family and schoolfriends will not do anything for him after Kes has died. But maybe Mr Farthing can? What do you think?

YOUTH EMPLOYMENT OFFICER

The Youth Employment Officer only appears once in the book, but he is important in several ways. He interviews Billy for career advice, totally fails to give him any, and the meeting ends when Billy, realizing that Kes may be in danger, rushes off (pp. 137–40).

You may have a clear picture in your mind of what the Youth Employment Officer looks like (balding) and you might even imagine him talking in a particular way, using a particular accent.

What is he like as a person? He certainly seems abrupt and sharp when he speaks to Billy. He obviously doesn't understand the sort of person Billy is, or realize, either, that although Billy isn't up to taking exams he doesn't want to go down the pit. In fact, he has very little interest in finding out what Billy is good at or what he wants to do. Write down some examples of things the Youth Employment Officer says or does that show what he is like as a person, then write them out as a description of him.

The main reason for the officer's importance to the book is that he shows us something about Billy's future. Up to now, Billy has been able to ignore the problem of what he is going to do after school. The teachers (except Farthing) don't seem to talk about it and his family don't care. Here is someone from outside actually telling Billy that he will probably end up down the pit. Also, we realize that no one is actually going to help Billy. All the officer can give him is a leaflet. How does all this affect the way we feel about Billy – particularly at the end of the book when Kes is dead?

Finally, Barry Hines uses the Youth Employment Officer to point out faults he finds with school – particularly in the way people are helped to choose jobs. What things do you think Barry Hines is criticizing when he includes a character like the Youth Employment Officer?

SUGDEN

We meet Sugden, the frustrated football player turned games master, when he takes Billy for a games lesson, bullies him throughout the match and then attacks him afterwards in revenge for Billy's losing the match for him.

You should have a fairly clear picture in your mind of how Sugden looks and sounds, but, if not, read through sections 16 and 17 and jot down words to remind you.

When you have a good image of him, try to understand what Sugden is like. He has obviously been good at football in his time, but possibly not good enough. What do you think happened? What was his early career as a footballer like, and why didn't it work out for him?

Now he is teaching. Does he enjoy his job, and is he a good teacher? Does he remind you of any games teacher you've ever had – is he different or the same? Compare Sugden with the other teachers in the book – Crossley, Gryce and Farthing – and decide whether he is better or worse.

Sugden is not a very nice person. Pick out the three worst things Sugden says or does. Now imagine you are the teacher and Sugden the pupil. What would you say to him about the things he has said or done? How would you explain to him why he shouldn't do them again?

Finally, think about what Sugden actually adds to the book. Does he make it more interesting, and if so, how? Perhaps he tells us about Billy's character. Perhaps he adds comedy to the book. Imagine Sugden wasn't in the book at all; what would be missing?

GRYCE

Gryce, Billy's headmaster, is the worst possible example of what a headmaster should be. We first meet him, at a distance, taking morning assembly. When he sees Billy daydreaming, he punishes him. Later in the book, when Billy misses the Youth Employment interview, Gryce tells him off again.

We do not have a clear impression of what Gryce looks like, though he probably has a voice that gets people's attention. But we do have a good idea of the way he behaves.

The most obvious thing about him is that he rules with violence. Find three examples of things he does or says which show this. What effect do they have on the boys? Gryce canes and bullies his way through the day, and in the end, as he says, it doesn't make any difference. So why do you think Gryce continues to be violent?

Another thing about Gryce which makes him a poor headmaster is the fact that he does not even like the boys. What does the word 'disillusioned' mean? Do you think it describes Gryce?

The boys certainly do not like their headmaster. Write down some words they use about him in the book which show you how they feel. Do you think the other teachers like him? Does Sugden? Does Farthing? Do you think Sugden and Farthing have different ideas about Gryce?

It is useful to compare your own ideas about headmasters with Barry Hines's ideas. Have you ever met a headmaster as bad as Gryce – if not, do you think Barry Hines is exaggerating when he describes Gryce? What reasons might he have for making Gryce a larger-than-life villain? What does Gryce as villain add to the book?

SCHOOL FRIENDS

Billy's particular school friends up to the time he had Kes were MacDowall and Tibbut. They were going to go birds' nesting with him the day he found Kes. By the time the book starts they have fallen out with each other, because Billy spends so much time with Kes.

MacDowall is a bully and a troublemaker. Read particularly the part of the book where he and some others bully the messenger into hiding their smoking gear for them, and the part where he and Billy fight. What sort of a person do you think MacDowall is?

Tibbut, who is in Billy's class, seems to be good at sport. He is the captain of the football team in the games lesson, and is obviously used to this. He doesn't seem too keen on Billy either. He mocks him during the English lesson, and tells Jud where to find Billy when Jud is out for revenge.

The other members of Billy's class do not seem to take to him too much either. He gets laughed at when he calls out a wrong name at registration, and mocked when he starts to talk about Kes. Billy is seen as a class clown and a bit odd. He is a troublemaker who does not run with the pack.

Billy does not seem to have any friends in school. Why do you think this is? At one point there was certainly evidence that he was beginning to be more popular; think of two things that happen during the book that prove this. If you were in Billy's class, what could you say to help him to make more friends?

Themes

FAMILY LIFE

What do we mean by family life? When we think of a family, we often think of the advertisement image – a young mum and dad with two young children, living in a sparkling new house. Many families aren't like this – and in *Kes*, Barry Hines shows us one that definitely isn't.

Billy's family is not a happy one. It was broken up when he was still a child, and his mother was not strong enough to make a good home for Jud and Billy on her own. So the family life we see in the book is not contented. You can probably think of several details which show us that Billy's family is not well off. What sort of practical problems do they have? Billy doesn't have a warm, welcoming home to come back to – even at fifteen he has to fend for himself, buy his own food. His mum has other priorities.

There are emotional problems, too, in Billy's family. His mum is not interested in Billy or his brother. She can't control either of them, or give them security or affection. Think of ways in which she could make her relationship with them better. Jud, Billy's older brother, is even worse – he lives his own life, ignores his mum, and takes out his frustrations on his younger brother. Look at how Jud bullies Billy, and how Billy reacts to this. How could all this be improved?

Billy himself realizes that a lot of his problems come from the fact that his family does not support him. He really wants a happy family life. He gazes enviously at the houses on Firs Hill and the families who live there. Look particularly at the description on page 16 of how he peers through the letter-box. And when Billy is asked in school to write an imaginary story, he pictures a happy family life with lots of food, a mum who looks after him, and a dad who stays with him. We realize at the very end of the book that life started to go wrong for Billy when his dad left home. Read the section where Billy remembers how happy life was before that time, and how awful it was when his dad went away.

There is really no one who can provide support for Billy and take the place of his family. He doesn't have any friends. The school teachers for the most part don't seem to notice him, except when they tell him off. Only one person in the whole book gives Billy what a family – even a father – might give him: interest, support, encouragement. Who is this?

Because he doesn't have a family to help him, Billy loves Kes. Kes becomes his family. What does Billy get from and give to Kes that people can get from their family? Do you think this is enough for Billy? What doesn't he get from Kes – conversation, for example that might help him? Of course, when Kes is killed, this is as terrible for Billy as when his family was destroyed. Why do you think that it is at this point that Billy particularly remembers going to the pictures with his dad? It is cruel that Kes is taken away from Billy by a member of his own family, and that neither Jud nor his mum, who should be closest to him, understand how much the bird means to him.

What message is Barry Hines giving us about family life? First, of course, that it is not always happy. Lots of us know this, but maybe it is good to be reminded of how awful family life can be. Collect examples from the book of the bad things in Billy's family life.

Perhaps the second message is that it is possible to survive (Billy does, particularly when he has Kes), but that an unhappy family life does affect people. Do you agree with this idea? Do you think Billy's family caused his problems? Write a paragraph explaining your view, and saying in what ways Billy might have been different if he had a different family.

It is always interesting to see what differences and similarities there are between the way authors write about events and situations and the way we experience them. You might like to think of families you know, and compare them with Billy's family.

Do the families you know ever argue? Think of other ways they have of handling disagreements. Do the people in the family ever get unhappy and depressed? Do they take it out on other members of their family? Do they find other ways to cope? Think – as Billy does in the book – of the most ideal family you can imagine, and ask yourself how they would react if their son tamed a kestrel. This might help you see clearly how

Billy's family reacts and judge for yourself how bad – or good – this reaction is.

EDUCATION

'Schooldays are the happiest days of your life.' They certainly are not for Billy. He hates school and school seems to hate him. The main message about school Barry Hines conveys to us in *Kes* is that school is often a useless place that does not prepare children for life outside and only succeeds in making them miserable. Do you agree?

The first thing you may notice is that when Barry Hines describes the outside or inside of school – before he even starts talking about the people or the classes – we get a sense of boredom. Read the section beginning on page 126 where Jud chases Billy round the school, or even the part where Billy is waiting for his interview. Everything is dull, vandalized, ugly. How does this differ from the descriptions of fields, woods, Kes? What is Barry Hines telling us?

When we start meeting the people in the school, it gets worse. Of the four teachers we meet, three of them are insensitive bullies. Crossley is unsympathetic, with no sense of humour. Sugden is sarcastic, cruel and self-centred. He has no love for teaching, only for showing himself off as a footballer. Gryce is a tyrant, who has worked his way up the teaching ladder to be head without learning anything about children or even liking them. The only way he knows is cruelty.

The general comment Barry Hines makes is that teachers like this should not be allowed near pupils. For example, how many examples can you find in the book of plain cruelty by teachers? How many times when a kind word or a bit of understanding would have helped?

Of course, the teachers get the results they deserve. Gryce admits he's getting nowhere – 'There's been no advance at all in discipline, decency, manners or morals' (p. 56). Billy agrees with him when he talks to Mr Farthing. So we see a school where, firstly, the boys do not learn. Billy admits he can hardly read or write. The lower ability classes, like 4C, are labelled idiots, and so they act like idiots.

We also have a school where violence is normal. All the teachers rule by violence – so it spreads to the boys, and we have bullying and fights.

MacDowall turns on Billy, the boys in his class back Sugden when he turns on the cold shower – even Mr Farthing resorts to physical means to teach MacDowall a lesson.

But there are some good things about the school. Barry Hines was a teacher himself, and he obviously rates highly some of the things that go on in schools.

The best person in Billy's school is Mr Farthing. He is a good teacher – Billy says he actually tries to teach the boys, even though they are in the lower ability band – and he is interested in them. We see him both with the class and with Billy; in control, not letting anyone get laughed at or bullied, yet taking them all seriously. Why is Farthing the best teacher in the school?

Sometimes the boys themselves turn against what is happening. They listen, fascinated, when Anderson and Billy tell their stories. They get really involved in the English lesson, the football match. In the end they refuse to go along with Sugden's bullying.

If you were appointed head of the school, how would you improve it? Don't just think of obvious ideas, like banning caning – be a bit out of the ordinary. How can you create a situation where people want to learn and can do this in the best way possible?

The final test of whether a school has provided a good education is whether the people who leave it are ready to cope with life outside. Billy is not. It is obvious from his interview with the Youth Employment Officer that he has gained nothing from his time in school except a very little literacy and a lot of beatings. And even the interview doesn't help him cope. It is worse than useless as a means of finding him a job. In what way has Billy's education made things worse for him? Think further than the obvious ways – like not teaching him to read and write. Think how school has bored him, encouraged him to turn to violence, made him lose all the confidence he should have had in life and in himself.

Look back over your education. Remember the schools or maybe colleges you have been to. See the buildings, the classrooms, the teachers. Hear their voices. Think of the others in your class. Were these experiences good or bad? Were they a mixture? Pick out the good bits, and the bits you would like to change. Now compare your education with Billy's. Has it been better or worse?

NATURE

Billy's life seems split into three parts – his life at home, his life at school, and that part of his life which is spent experiencing nature with Kes. It is this part which is the best, where he actually does enjoy himself, learns something and gives something back.

Billy lives on an estate – it is all brick and concrete, and even where plants and flowers have sprung up they are dying or have already been destroyed. Billy obviously hates these surroundings. We can tell this by the way Barry Hines describes them. But read any one of the descriptions of Billy in the fields and woods beyond the estate – delivering the papers, for example, or birds' nesting. It is obvious that Billy loves being in the country. Notice the details Barry Hines gives us. Jot down words and ideas which really describe what Billy is seeing, hearing, feeling. Even in the school toilets, for example, Billy can blow amazing bubbles and see beauty in them.

He has always loved animals. Billy tells Mr Farthing he has kept lots of birds – magpies and jackdaws – and other animals, like a fox cub. What sort of problems do you imagine he has had in rearing them? On the other hand, he has obviously learnt a lot. Read the section in which Billy is the only person who can get the dog off the football pitch during the games lesson, and write notes on what this shows you about him. He is obviously a natural with animals, and he also has a lot of skill.

But, as Billy says to Mr Farthing, the creature that means most to him is Kes. We see the whole development of their relationship – Billy finding Kes, bringing her home, rearing and training her, letting her free and keeping her. Then we have Billy's description of Kes flying to the lure and, later, the moving scene where Billy shows Mr Farthing this amazing sight.

What does Billy get from keeping Kes? Read this list, add any other things you feel are important, and then discuss it with other people. Arrange the list in order of importance. If you think the most important thing Billy gets from Kes is confidence, put that first. You may not agree with some of the ideas; if you don't, then leave them out.

1. Kes is a friend for Billy.
2. Kes takes the place of Billy's family.
3. Billy feels love for Kes.

4. Billy learns how to read better because of Kes.
5. With Kes, Billy has confidence.
6. Billy is skilful in handling Kes.
7. He has achieved something in training Kes and this gives him pride.
8. Billy enjoys working with Kes.
9. Billy has learned more about animals through being with Kes.
10. Kes makes Billy feel someone needs him.
11. Billy feels he is strong and powerful when he is with Kes.
12. Kes gives Billy a reason for living.
13. Billy is trapped – Kes can fly free, and this makes Billy feel better.

It is important we realize that Billy gives a lot to Kes as well. He certainly gives her affection – and as you will know if you've read the section of this book on training hawks (pp. 79–80), has also had to be committed to her all the time. Find three things that Billy has to do as a result of looking after Kes. Then write a paragraph beginning 'Billy gives Kes . . .' Do you think you would be able to give this much to an animal or bird you were looking after?

And so, when Kes goes, Billy's life falls apart. We never really know how Billy feels, but we can guess from his actions that from the moment he suspects (in the Youth Employment interview), he is desperate. Notice how he runs out to the fields, then through the woods – and how these are described very clearly. Why do you think Barry Hines describes Billy's run so carefully? What might he be saying to us?

Kes is dead – and part of Billy's life is, too. Because Kes was so important to him, when Kes goes Billy shuts the door on all that part of his life. After challenging Jud and his mum (and literally throwing Kes in their faces), Billy goes out again – but this time, not to the countryside. He has finished with all that. He cannot bear to touch it again. He goes through the estate and the town – and this tells us a lot about where his life is going now. Read the two descriptions: of his run through the woods and his walk through the town to the cinema. How do these two descriptions differ? What are we meant to feel when reading each of them?

Perhaps you do not sympathize with Billy. Perhaps you prefer the city to nature and the countryside. If so, write an account of a walk in the city that makes it seem beautiful. You don't have to agree with Billy's viewpoint, or with Barry Hines's. But whether you agree with Billy or not, it is certainly sad that at the end of *Kes* he writes off that part of his life. Perhaps the important point here is that Billy goes home and puts Kes's body in the bin before going to bed. What does this show us? What might Kes stand for? So what is Billy putting in the bin?

RIGHT AND WRONG

There are lots of things in *Kes* which can be seen as wrong – but it all depends on your point of view. Certainly Barry Hines is asking us to question what is right and wrong. What do you think?

What about Billy – is he good or bad? He has been in trouble with the police, and he still steals occasionally. Is this to get his own back on people, or just because he is hungry? But is he a villain, like Jud? To help you decide, look at this list of some of the things Billy does that could be called wrong. For each, write one sentence beginning: 'Billy was wrong to do this because . . .', and one starting: 'Billy was not wrong to do this because . . .'

1. Nearly knocking Mr Porter off his ladder.
2. Stealing the library book.
3. Hitting Jud when he was drunk.
4. Daydreaming in assembly.
5. Taking a kestrel chick to rear.
6. Lying to Sugden.
7. Letting the goal in during the football match.
8. Answering his mother back.

Now read through what you've written and decide which of the things Billy did really are wrong.

What would Billy say about each of them? How would he defend himself? Does this make any difference to what you think?

Now think of five things Billy does that you think are 'good'. Does this make any difference to how you think of him? In particular, imagine how Mr Farthing might describe Billy after seeing him fly Kes. Does this description tie in with what other people think of him? And in a way, however bad Billy is, he is not completely to blame, for he is influenced by other people – at school and at home.

Think about Billy's school. There, Gryce says most of the things the boys do are wrong – coughing before a hymn, smoking, daydreaming. The teachers punish Billy for not listening, not understanding, not having P.E. kit. Do you think all these are wrong? Are some more dangerous than others? Do you think people should be punished for them?

On the other hand, a lot of the teachers use violence in school. They cane pupils. They cuff them round the head. They put them under the cold shower and won't let them out. Are these things wrong? Are they worse or better than the actions they are punishing?

Write a list of the people Billy knows at school – the four teachers, the two boys. Alongside each of them, put down the things they did in the book that could be thought of as wrong. Use the list below, adding any other actions you can think of: you can use the same words for more than one person.

beat Billy	teased Billy
bullied MacDowall	caned boys for no reason
told Billy off	smoked
humiliated Billy	cheated
bullied Billy	wanted to be the centre of
fought with Billy	attention
put Billy in the cold shower	

Now consider whether in fact you think what these people have done is wrong. Maybe it was just silly, or they couldn't help it. Choose two people from the list, one who you think is good, one who you think is bad, and write down your thoughts about them.

In general, what do you think of Billy's school – does it encourage boys to consider what is right or wrong? Has it influenced Billy for better or for worse?

Billy's family, Jud and his mum, seem just as violent as the teachers. Jud is a villain who bets, bullies Billy and gets drunk. His mum has lots of boyfriends, doesn't look after Billy, isn't really interested in him. Certainly none of these things is illegal – and there are no teachers around to punish Jud or his mum.

But perhaps Jud and his mum are actually worse than the people at school. Can you think of why they may be more to blame? What pressures are they under? In many ways, they influence Billy to be just like they are – so are they even more to blame than the teachers? And in the end, the ultimate wrong action – the death of Kes – is due to a member of Billy's family.

In fact when Jud kills Kes, Billy appeals to his mum to punish Jud – but she can't, simply because Jud is bigger than she is.

In school, one set of rules applies; outside, whoever is strongest does what he likes. This is not fair – but it is what happens.

If you could re-write the last part of the book so that what you think to be the 'right thing' actually happened, how would it end? Would Jud be punished? Perhaps Billy would get another hawk? Write about how you would alter this part of the book so that right won out in the end.

Background Information

HAWK CONSERVANCY

Perhaps one of the best and most accessible ways to see what Billy and Mr Farthing saw when Kes flew is to go to Great Britain's only Hawk Conservancy and see a flying display. Situated in the countryside near Andover in Hampshire, the Conservancy used to be a wildlife park, established by Reg Smith in 1965, and was turned over to work solely with birds of prey in 1980.

If you arrive just before any of the four flying displays that are held every day from March to October, you will usually find an interested group of people – or an excited school party – waiting near the flying ground. This is a large grass area bounded by hedges and trees, with seats where you can sit to watch the display.

On the particular autumn day described here, it was Ashley, Reg's son, who brought the birds out. First, there was a Harris hawk called George, who eyed everyone confidently as he sat on Ashley's gloved hand. As he was released he took off with a flurry of wings for the roof of the nearby outhouses, where he sat and enjoyed his freedom for a while. Ashley called him loudly, holding up a titbit of meat, and George came, circling, then flying straight as a rocket a few feet above the ground, to land unerringly on the glove and pick delicately at the meat.

Hawks like George, Ashley told the audience, are woodland birds. You can identify them by their long tails and rounded wings. They are the sprinters among the birds of prey, flying short distances, dropping quickly and accurately. Everyone had a turn at flying George, putting on the protective glove against the razor-sharp talons, then holding up the meat and calling. He came every time, condescended to take the meat, then flew straight to Ashley for more.

Next it was the turn of a Lannar falcon called Peggy. Unlike hawks, the short-tailed pointed-winged falcons work the hedgerows, looking for prey, and they will pursue their quarry for four or five miles if necessary. The other animals and birds know this. As soon as Peggy was released the skies cleared of birds and presumably the hedgerows cleared of wildlife. Unlike George, Peggy is a one-man bird. She will only work with Ashley, so it was he who swung the lure and called her until she came swooping down towards it. At the last moment Ashley turned it away from the falcon, so that she flew past – a game that lasted, swoop after swoop, for all too short a time. Then, with a shout that let Peggy know that at last she would be successful, Ashley let her take the lure, catching it in her talons and bearing it to the ground. She immediately mantled her wings over it – to protect it from other birds of prey – and began eating.

The last bird to fly was a kestrel, brought to everyone in the audience to hold on gloved hands. Small and delicate, it eyed everyone shyly and curiously, as if wondering what they were doing there. The kestrel, Ashley told the audience, is the most common indigenous bird of prey in Great Britain – and it can be found in every country in the world. Whereas many hawks are like jet aeroplanes, the kestrel is a helicopter, hovering over the land for long periods, looking for rodents and field mice – until suddenly it stoops like a stone to its prey. It has successfully learnt to live with humans, nesting (as in *Kes*) on buildings such as high-rise blocks of flats. Some have even nested in Salisbury Cathedral.

And then the display was at an end. As a bonus, we were allowed to look around the Hawk Conservancy. Here, in aviaries, were the birds – hawks, owls, falcons, eagles and vultures of all kinds.

Ashley talked enthusiastically about the work of the Conservancy. As well as mounting flying displays, it takes in injured birds for recovery and release. It cares for those who cannot go back to the wild. It breeds birds of prey to increase Britain's supply, and has exchange schemes with many of the world's zoos. Plans are also under way for a museum.

In addition, the Conservancy is keen to help increase people's understanding of birds of prey and so it runs a full education programme for schools.

'There are those who think falconry is a cruel sport,' said Ashley, 'but maybe they don't realize that birds kill in the wild anyway. It's nature's way of making sure species are strong. The strong survive, the weak and the slow get killed by others – like the birds of prey.' And does everyone think that? No. 'The main problem,' said Ashley, 'are those people who think they can do it themselves. We have many cases of young birds being brought to us abandoned, having been taken from the nest by people who want to rear and train them.'

Perhaps you think falconry is cruel? If so, write down your opinions, remembering what Ashley had to say.

What do you feel about people who want to train hawks themselves – like Billy, in *Kes*? What would you say to a friend who told you he had found a hawk's nest and was going to take a chick?

Having read about the Hawk Conservancy and about the training of a hawk in the section that follows, think again about the book, *Kes*. Can you think of any dangers in writing a book about a young boy training a hawk? Can you think of any ways to offset the dangers?

TRAINING A HAWK

Using birds to fly and catch prey in a controlled way is as old as many of the ancient civilizations. As you can tell from the quotation at the beginning of *Kes*, by the Middle Ages the practice was so well established in England that various ranks used different birds. In those days, hunting with hawks was more than a game; it was the best way of catching fresh bird-meat to eat.

When guns were invented, falconry slowly became less important, and now exists in Great Britain as a highly skilled and developed sport with its own clubs and societies. The largest society is the British Falconers' Club, with over a thousand members, which publishes its own annual journal, *The Falconer*, and holds regular flying meetings and courses.

Reading *Kes*, you might be tempted to think that training a hawk is simply a matter of finding a chick and feeding it until it grows into an adult. It is not as easy as that, though.

In order to be a falconer – that is, to fly a hunting hawk, as Billy did – members have to be sure they can keep and feed their hawk properly, handle it, train it and provide it with prey. 'A hawk, unlike a gun or a fishing rod,' says the hand-out, 'can't be stored in a cupboard when unwanted.' When someone takes on the training of, for example, a kestrel, they may be committing themselves to ten years of hard work. A falconer normally keeps a kestrel for its lifetime. All the things that Billy did – feeding Kes, obtaining food for her, rushing home at lunchtime to fly her – have to be done every day, with no breaks. Many falconers have had no proper holiday for ten or fifteen years at a stretch, simply because of the problems of leaving their hawk.

If members can prove that they can commit themselves to caring for a hawk, and that their situation is suitable for providing prey – for example, few people living in towns qualify – then the B.F.C. will support them in the long training to become a falconer. It is usual to begin with a bird such as a buzzard, and to choose a bird suitable to the area around you so that it can catch the food it needs. Most people in Great Britain fly hawks, which are more suited to woodland, than falcons, which prefer open spaces.

To obtain a hawk for training, it is possible to buy one bred in captivity or to take one from the wild under a special licence. A recent law (the Wildlife and Countryside Act, 1981) actually makes it illegal to do what Billy did and simply steal from a nest or take a bird from the wild, and there are severe and expensive penalties for breaking this law. (You might like to consider why strict laws have been introduced.) Once a bird has been obtained, it has to be ringed and registered with the Department of the Environment, and after that a watch is kept to make sure the bird is being treated properly.

Having obtained his bird, the falconer then works hard to rear it, feeding it carefully, watching for the slightest sign of illness which can kill a bird within hours, making sure he develops a good relationship with it. As it grows he begins to train it, getting it used to flying on a creance, gradually encouraging it until it is ready to fly free, hunt, kill and then return to him. The relationship between falconer and bird is special and comes from the discipline, patience and commitment of years.

All this – licensing, registering, training – is very different from what happens in *Kes*. It seems unromantic, but in fact it is realistic. You might like to write down some of the problems a person might encounter if they didn't know how to train a hawk. Consider, too, who will suffer most if the hawk isn't cared for properly – the owner or the hawk.

If you are particularly interested in falconry, contact the British Falconers' Club, Moonrakers, Allington, Salisbury SP4 0EX.

Passages for Comparison

The way Barry Hines has written about Kes is not the only way to describe birds. Many other people have taken as their inspiration the wonder of birds (hunting birds in particular), flight and falconry. It is interesting to compare some of the ways other people have written about these things with how Barry Hines has done it. Look particularly at the words these authors use, the images they create, the way the words sound. Barry Hines has written his novel in prose, but other authors have often felt it more appropriate to use the rhyme and rhythm of poetry to express their ideas about birds.

Use these extracts in many different ways. Read them through and enjoy them. Understand the words and ideas they include, perhaps by discussing them with friends. Think about the ways in which each author's view of birds differs from Barry Hines's. Then compare the words, sounds, images, rhyme and rhythm of the language in these extracts with the language in *Kes*.

You can write about these things, too. Start by concentrating on what birds mean to you. What pictures do you have when you think of them? What sounds come to your mind? What sensations, what feelings, do you experience? They might be positive – triumphant, full of movement – or a little disturbing. Let these thoughts lead to words, then write these words down. At first, simply write, grouping your words in a way that looks, sounds and feels right to you. Afterwards, pay attention to whether the words are spelt correctly and the sentences put together logically.

Remember that your ideas about birds, flight and hunting are just as important as those of the authors of these pieces of writing – or of Barry Hines.

THE BIRD

Adventurous bird walking upon the air,
Like a schoolboy running and loitering, leaping and springing,
Pensively pausing, suddenly changing your mind
To turn at ease on the heel of a wing-tip. Where
In all the crystalline world was there to find
For your so delicate walking and airy winging
A floor so perfect, so firm and so fair,
And where a ceiling and walls so sweetly ringing
Whenever you sing, to your clear singing?

The wind-winged soul itself can ask no more
Than such pure, resilient and endless floor
For its strong-pinioned plunging and soaring and upward and upward
   springing!

Edwin Muir

BUZZARD SOARING

So long grounded

in himself, under such
feather weight

he seems to rise
out of a sack.

A dead poundage
re-assembles on the wings

Spread into a sycamore key
turning. Earth breathes him out,

exhales him from his vantage,
to glide with the traffic between worlds,

the exploding galaxies of spores,
the achenes suspended in their shrouds

The equality, the lightness here . . .
He feels his shadow separate

and travel the air, another
wanderer, another dust.

Below, history fires its
intricate acreage. Demesnes melt.

Towns bleed across ploughland.
Motorways grub like glaciers.

He suns. He sleepwalks on the wing
through this world and the next,

hearing the hormones hiss, hearing
the froth in his cells: Re-enter

the inferno. Rise again as ash.

Roger Garfitt

THE HAWK IN THE RAIN

I drown in the drumming ploughland, I drag up
Heel after heel from the swallowing of the earth's mouth,
From clay that clutches my each step to the ankle
With the habit of the dogged grave, but the hawk

Effortlessly at height hangs his still eye.
His wings hold all creation in a weightless quiet,
Steady as a hallucination in the streaming air.
While banging wind kills these stubborn hedges,

Thumbs my eyes, throws my breath, tackles my heart,
And rain hacks my head to the bone, the hawk hangs
The diamond point of will that polestars
The sea drowner's endurance: and I,

Bloodily grabbed dazed last-moment-counting
Morsel in the earth's mouth, strain towards the master-
Fulcrum of violence where the hawk hangs still.
That maybe in his own time meets the weather

Coming the wrong way, suffers the air, hurled upside down,
Fall from his eye, the ponderous shires crash on him,
The horizon trap him; the round angelic eye
Smashed, mix his heart's blood with the mire of the land.

                                                    Ted Hughes

THE GOSHAWK

And then, suddenly, Cully had seen. I felt her murderous feet tighten on the glove. We stood together, staring at the eye motionless. Our veins coalesced, and the blood ran in a circuit through both of us. I could feel Cully's blood wondering whether she was to be checked and whether she could kill despite her feathers: she could feel mine in terror.

'Go then, Cully,' I said.

And by God's grace, Cully went.

The moment that the wings flicked out, the rabbit went too. We were between him and his home, so he had to run toward Three Parks Wood, which was fifty yards away on the other side. He had a start of ten yards and his pursuer was a cripple. As soon as one had flown the hawk one felt as if virtue had gone out of one, as if life was being lived elsewhere. One became a spectator suddenly. It looked as if the rabbit would make the wood.

But he lived on this side. He did not know what sanctuary he would find away from us, and he was determined on breaking back. The ragged wings were after him, were within a yard, and my heart was praying encouragement and advice, begging her to strike now. It was like being an onlooker at an athletic meeting who kicks to help the highjumper. The talons were within a foot; and the rabbit squatted.

Cully shot over him, tried vainly to stop herself with the half a dozen shattered feathers of her tail, and landed on the empty ground. Her quarry was on his feet at once, streaking straight back to me. Cully ran after him, bounding like a kangaroo. It was horrible to see the creature which ought to be able to fly, running pathetically after him with a leaping gait. But she gained flying-speed, managed to get into the air. I ran, waving at the rabbit, to head him off; could see the bird's yellow eye boiling with fire. The rabbit turned sideways to run round me. She grazed his back. Landed. He turned again, but she turned with him. It was hop, skip, jump. She was there!

I took out my hunting knife and was with them in half a dozen paces. It was a long-bladed sheath-knife, and very sharp. She held him down, quite powerless, with one great talon on his loins and the other on his shoulders. I put the point of my knife between his ears, and pressed downward, pinning the split skull to the ground.

T. H. White

THE KESTREL

Kestrels can often be tricky to get feeding from the fist, and much patience is required to overcome this reluctance. I have found it a good idea to take the bird and its food indoors on the fist, and then to ignore it unless it bates. I sit and watch television or read a book, while the bird makes up its own mind that I am not going to hurt it as soon as it turns its attention away from me. Sooner or later, it will start to pull at the meat, but if it is really stubborn, leave it with its food on its block and watch from a discreet distance until it starts to eat – which it invariably will as soon as you are out of sight – and then, after it has consumed a few mouthfuls, go and pick it up with the meat. Usually it will continue to eat almost immediately, for having got the taste of the meat it will be unable to resist the temptation. As soon as the bird is feeding readily from the fist, you should start weighing it daily, keeping a record of both the weight of the bird and the weight of its food. Kestrels normally need three-quarters to one ounce of meat each day, to keep them at a steady weight, and slightly less to drop them to flying-weight, but these amounts are only approximate since each bird is different.

Once your bird is feeding from the fist with confidence, the next step is to get it jumping. Initially, this may be done while it is still tethered to its block. The aim is to get it to jump a couple of inches to take a piece of meat from your fist. The best method is to crouch on the ground with your side towards the bird, and your gloved hand outstretched a few inches above the height of the block. Hold the meat firmly between your thumb and forefinger and encourage the kestrel to jump towards you. It may be necessary to attract the bird's attention by wiggling the meat, tapping your fist with a finger of your other hand, and whistling softly. Do not allow your fist to stray close enough to the kestrel to let it snatch the meat or it will spend the next ten minutes leaning precariously off the block while trying to grab the meat without jumping. It is advisable to cut a kestrel's meat into long slivers so that they can be swallowed in one, or easily pulled to pieces. Kestrels are fussy eaters, and if the pieces are too large or too tough they will spend ages, however keen they are, picking delicately at their meat in an infuriating manner.

Once a kestrel will come approximately six feet instantly to the fist, it can be introduced to the lure. The meat tied on to the lure may either be a large enough chunk to allow the bird to pull off mouthfuls each time it catches the lure, or a series of small pieces that can be consumed immediately and then replaced for the next flight. The first step in this new stage of the training is to get the kestrel to associate the lure with food. Introduce the lure while your kestrel is on its block on the weathering ground. Drop the lure, with the meat firmly attached, on to the ground next to the block. By twitching the lure to draw attention to the meat, encourage the bird to hop down and eat from the lure. Repeat the process until the kestrel bates at the lure as soon as it is produced. When it is thus showing instant recognition of the lure, move the training session back to the flying ground again. Hold the lure stick in your gloved hand and the lure line in the other, then drop the lure on the ground a few feet from the flying post. If the kestrel ignores it, either pick it up and drop it again, or jerk the lure to attract the bird's attention, being careful to ensure that the meat is easily visible. When the kestrel lands on the lure, keep hold of the lure line, keep your foot on the creance, and 'make in' – meaning crouch down on the ground

and edge slowly towards the bird, so as not to frighten it. If it does take fright, it may try to fly off, with or without the lure. If it flies away with the lure, this can become a vice later on known as 'carrying', when the bird, flying free, catches the lure and attempts to fly off with it to eat it in a more secluded place – a particularly irritating habit which can be avoided by correct management in the early stages. As you reach the kestrel, you should have ready in your fist a piece of meat which serves as a pick-up piece. Place your fist over the lure and encourage the bird to step up, taking the jesses and putting the lure in your bag. Replace the bird on its post and gradually increase the distance until it is coming quickly from about fifteen yards. Now try hanging the lure about eight inches above the ground; if the kestrel lands on the ground below the meat, rather than taking it in flight, lower the meat so that it can reach

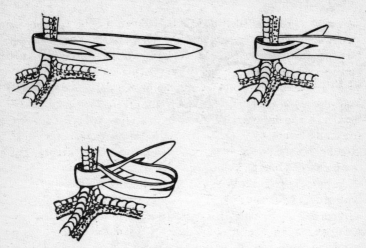

up to it. As it does this, drop the lure on to the ground so that it can take the food, and make in. Eventually, or you may have been lucky first time, the kestrel will hit the lure as it hangs in mid-air. Again, drop the line immediately so that it can take the meat. Once it is coming quickly from fifty yards and taking the lure in the air, you can start swinging the lure and trying to get your bird to make a pass. You begin this next stage in training by pulling the lure out of the bird's flight

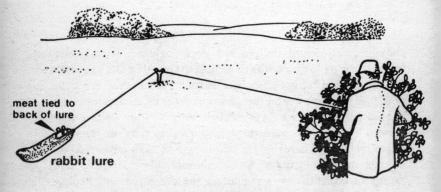

meat tied to
back of lure

rabbit lure

In *Kes* Billy used a lure that he whirled around his head. This is another way of using a lure to fly a kestrel.

path as it approaches. Try to avoid having trees behind you, since a kestrel will often head straight for a tree as soon as the lure is removed from its path. In open ground a kestrel will either come to land somewhere beyond you, or, and this is what you are hoping for, fly on a short distance and turn back towards the lure. On the second approach, it should be allowed to take the lure on the ground. When the bird is turning back to the lure it is ready to be flown free. When flying a bird free for the first time it is advisable to have someone else present to help keep the bird in sight should something go wrong. Never fly your kestrel free for the first time on its initial flight of the day; always give it a flight to the lure on the creance first. Call it off a slightly shorter distance for the first free flight, and make in slowly as usual when it is on the lure.

From now on it is simply a matter of working the bird to increase the number of stoops to the lure, but take things gently and allow the bird to catch the lure – on the ground or, preferably, in the air – as soon as it shows signs of tiring. When you intend the kestrel to take the lure in the air, swing the lure faster and throw it upwards to encourage the bird to climb to take it. It may miss the lure and follow it down to the ground, but this is only an error in timing on the bird's part, and it will improve with practice. Most falconers use a call to indicate to the bird that it can take the lure the next time it comes in. The traditional call is 'Ho!' However, do not use the call every time you are going to let the bird catch the lure or it will soon get the habit of not coming unless it hears the call.

Emma Ford

Glossary

achene: pod
arabesque: curve
asphalt: tarred road or pavement
assimilation: absorption

bearings: directions
bevelled: rounded
buff: eddy

cartilage: gristle
chassé: dancing step
chaff: grain husks
coalesce: combine, fuse into one
composition: arrangement
converge: meet
covey: flock
cretin: idiot
crystalline: clear as crystal

demesnes: estates
deteriorate: get worse
dirge: lament
dray: cart
dubbin: polish

emanate: come
emulator: imitator
enunciate: pronounce
equidistant: equally distant
exhale: breathe out

façade: front of a building
feint: sham

fetter: shackle
flexion: movement
florin: two old shillings (ten new pence)
fluctuation: rise and fall
foliage: greenery
fulcrum: point of balance, pivot

gouge: cut out
grub: dig

haphazard: casual
hasp: fastening
hawker: salesman
hawking: clearing throat
hawser: cable

impetus: force
ineptitude: clumsiness
inferno: hell, hot place
initially: at first
interlude: pause
intricate: complicated

jack: lift
jamb: door post

laterally: to the side
lath: thin piece of wood
lintels: stone or wood over a door
lubricate: make slippery

mash: brew

masonry: stonework
medley: mixed company
membrane: skin
mesmeric: hypnotic
midget: dwarf
misdemeanour: misdeed
momentum: impetus, movement
monotone: single unchanging tone
mooching: slouching
mythical: legendary

nog: block
nucleus: core

oblivion: end
ornithology: study of birds

parabola: curve
paraphernalia: belongings
pendant: hanging
pensively: thoughtfully
peregrinations: travels
perimeter: edge
peripheral: on the edge
permeate: saturate
peruse: read carefully
peter: fade
pigmentation: colouring
pinion: wing
plane: glide, sweep
plantain: flat-leaved plant
plus-fours: wide trousers ending below knee
polestars: gives direction, as the polestar guides sailors
portal: gate
poundage: weight, charge
precarious: uncertain
precede: go before
prematurely: hastily, very early
premises: buildings

reprobate: wicked character
resilient: elastic
riding: track
rufous: reddish-brown

scythe: cut down
secluded: private
sidle: walk sideways
skiddle: slide back and forth
slick: make sleek
sliver: long thin slice
smirk: smile stupidly
snap: packed lunch
snicket: alley
sorrel: herb
spasmodic: in fits and starts
splendiferous: splendid
spore: seed
stance: position
stippling: shading by means of dots

tanner: six old pence ($2\frac{1}{2}$p)
tarsus: ankle bones
teem: overflow
tibia: shin
trajectory: curving path
travesty: mockery

undulating: wavy

vantage: viewpoint
variegated: irregular
vicinity: neighbourhood

wake: path
wax: get bigger
welcher: someone who doesn't pay a debt

zenith: highest point

TERMS IN FALCONRY

bate: fly off in a panic
creance: long line
eyas: young hawk not yet trained
flake: sharpen beak
gauntlet: thick, long-wristed glove
jesses: leather straps put round a
    hawk's legs

lure: decoy to call a hawk
mute: faeces
prey: animal hunted for killing
primaries: first feathers
stoop: to drop onto prey
swivel: ring and pivot

Discussion Topics and Examination Questions

DISCUSSION TOPICS

Your understanding and appreciation of the novel will be much increased if you discuss aspects of it with other people. Here are some of the topics you can consider (some may have been considered during the course of this Passnote, but concentrate again here on their importance):

1. Work out exactly what *you* feel about Billy. Consider how far you sympathise with him and also aspects of his behaviour which you would condemn.
2. Which incident do you find the saddest in the novel and why?
3. Consider the view that Billy is trapped by his home and his school. In what ways does he succeed in escaping from them both?
4. Do you find Barry Hines's view of life pessimistic? Consider certain incidents which either support or contradict this idea.
5. There is plenty of comedy in the novel. What, for you, is the funniest sequence in the book and why?
6. Look closely at the part played in the novel by either a member of Billy's family or by one of the teachers.
7. 'The real theme of the novel is loneliness.' How far do you agree or disagree with this statement?
8. How does Barry Hines create a particular atmosphere (for example, that of fear) in any part or parts of the story?
9. Kes comes to dominate Billy's life. How far do you think this is a good or bad thing? Why?
10. 'Billy is a natural outsider anyway.' How far do you agree with this judgement?
11. Does Barry Hines succeed in making his characters fully alive? You might consider Billy's Mum, Jud, Gryce and Sugden, for example.
12. Which sequence in *Kes* is the most exciting and why?

THE GCSE EXAMINATION

If you are studying for the GCSE examination you may find that the set texts have been selected by your teacher from a very wide list of suggestions in the examination syllabus. The questions in the examination paper will therefore be applicable to many different books. Here are some possible questions which you could answer by making use of *Kes*:

1. Write about an absorbing hobby or interest or dream which is important in a novel or story you have read.
2. Write an account of the leading character in your chosen book that shows what his attitudes are to misfortune and the challenges of life and education.
3. Write about anything in the book you are studying that deals with either the pressures of family and friends, or the situations in school.
4. Compare and contrast one of the good characters in a book you have studied with one of the bad.
5. Write about the picture of childhood which is given in a book you have read.
6. Give an account of a funny or grotesque or powerful or unusual character who appears in a book you have studied.
7. By a close look at your chosen book, show how the author creates an exciting or fearful or unpleasant atmosphere in any incident or incidents.
8. Write about any two or three conversations in a book you have read and show how lifelike (or un-lifelike) they are.
9. Write about the picture of life – the social scene – which is given in your chosen book, bringing out the main qualities. In what ways is it like our own time?
10. Show how sympathy and encouragement and understanding play an important part in your chosen book.
11. Give an account of the way relationship develops in a book you have read recently.
12. Give an account of an outsider or loner in a book you are reading.